OTHER WORKS
by Summer Brenner

FICTION

The Soft Room
Dancers and the Dance
One Minute Movies
I-5, A Novel of Crime, Transportation, and Sex
Nearly Nowhere
My Life in Clothes
Do You Ever Think of Me? (vol. 1)

NOVELS FOR YOUTH

Richmond Tales, Lost Secrets of the Iron Triangle
Ivy, Homeless in San Francisco
Oakland Tales, Lost Secrets of The Town

POETRY

Everyone Came Dressed as Water
From the Heart to the Center

The Missing Lover

Summer Brenner

COLLAGES BY LEWIS WARSH

Spuyten Duyvil
New York City

A theatrical version of *The Missing Lover* had three professional readings at Z Space Studio and New College in San Francisco. A special thanks to director Peter Glazer and actors Nancy Shelby (from Word for Word Performing Arts Company) and Dominic Riley.

The Missing Lover was originally published by Spuyten Duyvil in a limited writer-artist edition of fifty copies with collages by Lewis Warsh.

Excerpts from *A Love Story No, War* (also *YOU, A Love WAR Story*) were published in *J Weekly* and *Wreckage of Reason, An Anthology of Contemporary XXperimental Prose by Women Writers*, Spuyten Duyvil.

The Soft Room was first published by The Figures, 1978, 1983. Excerpts from *The Soft Room* appeared in The Foothill Quarterly and Yellow Silk; and the anthologies *American Poetry Since 1970: Up Late* (4 Walls 8 Windows); *Cradle and All* (Faber & Faber); *Deep Down: New Sensual Writing by Women* (Faber & Faber); and *The Erotic Impulse* (Tarcher/Perigree).

Included in the text of *The Soft Room* are lines from "Corrina, Corrina" by Bob Dylan; and in *A Love Story No, War* excerpts from *Inanna, Queen of Heaven and Earth, Her Stories and Hymns from Sumer* by Diane Wolkstein, Samuel Noah Kramer, Harper and Row, 1983.

©2022 Summer Brenner

ISBN 978-1-933132-28-0; ISBN 978-1-956005-50-9

Cover and collages © Lewis Warsh

Library of Congress Cataloging-in-Publication Data

Brenner, Summer.
The missing lover : three novellas / Summer Brenner.
p. cm.
ISBN-13: 978-1-933132-28-0
I. Title.

PS3552.R386M57 2007
813'.54--dc22
2006022049

for Michael

THE MISSING LOVER

A LOVE STORY NO, WAR

THE SOFT ROOM

FOREWORD

Love is a word, a four-letter word as Bob Dylan reminds us. A gift, a curse, a source of pleasure and pain, a longing, a path, a means and an end, abstract and concrete, active and passive, transcendent, legitimate, forbidden, sacred, elusive, palpable, with symbols of the heart, the stars, roses, rings, knots, the moon, there are almost endless ways to describe or qualify love. Greek categorizes specific kinds of love: *eros* as romance and passion; *philia* as friendship; *ludus* as flirtation; *storge* as commitment and loyalty; *philautia* as self-love; *pragma* as companionship; and *agápe* as universal empathy and love beyond self.

These stories attempt to capture three different kinds of love. *The Missing Lover* is about longing and memory. *A Love Story No, War* probes the limits of bonds and sacrifice. *The Soft Room* explores youthful rapture and recklessness. I hope you enjoy them.

We have all become people according to the measure in which we have loved people and have had occasion for loving.

—Boris Pasternak, *Safe Passage*

THE MISSING LOVER

Je suis belle, ô mortels! comme un rêve de pierre,
Et mon sein, où chacun s'est meurtri tour à tour,
Est fait pour inspirer au poète un amour
Éternel et muet ainsi que la matière.

I'm beautiful, O mortals! like a dream of stone;
My breasts, upon which, turn by turn, each one is killed,
Are fashioned so that love, with which the poet's filled,
Stays quiet and eternal as a fossil bone.

—Charles Baudelaire
from "La Beauté," *Les Fleurs du Mal*
translated by William H. Crosby

1

Sarah is in a hotel room in Paris, scribbling the way writers do when they travel, trying to wrestle fiction from fact. She crosses out words and starts from the last time she heard the music. She had walked into a downtown shop, looking for a new shade for her bedroom window. How the shop stayed in business was a mystery. Always empty, always the same pleasantly disinterested proprietor in a starched dress shirt, creased slacks, and polished oxfords, the radio tuned to the classical music station.

Albinoni's Adagio in G minor assailed her. Blade in the gut. Blow on the head. Strike. Smack. Violation. She mentally collapsed as the proprietor asked, May I help you? Miss, Miss, may I help you?

No! No!

Sarah sits in a hotel room in Paris, scribbling the way writers do when they are overly stimulated from travel. Finally, she has to admit that fiction is a crummy still-life. An imitation. Mutation. Fabrication. Distraction. She starts again. This time she'll tell the truth one sentence at a time. One impossible sentence after the other.

She was broke, spending her pension check almost immediately and waiting for the next one. Yes, the U.S. government gave her money to study as a way to support children of deceased war veterans. A little for books. A little for rent, food, cigarettes. She survived on bread, cheese, steak-frites, boiled eggs, sugared coffee, and Gitanes.

They met on a movie set at Boulogne-Billancourt where she'd answered a call for extras. Instructions: nice attire. She wore her heather-green wool suit and high boots. Even extras got attention. Her hair was braided and twisted like *palmiers*, eye makeup applied, fake pearls fastened around her neck. And then typical of extras' work, she sat around all day waiting to be called: small effort, long hours, bad pay.

Two young Frenchmen sat nearby while she read Turgenev's *A Sportsman's Notebook* (Hepburn translation). Staring and making an occasional remark in English. One was Eric, the other Jean-Claude. One Mediterranean, the other Nordic. Both handsome in slacks, blazers, ties. Jean-Claude, she recognized from the Metro. A dozen times she'd seen him. She wanted to tell him, but maybe she was wrong. In a city of millions, could it really be him?

Finally, they were led to the set. A bistro with a dozen tables and chairs. They sat as a threesome while real food was served. They weren't allowed to eat, only smile and chat while they fiddled with forks and knives. Strictly ambiance.

It was a relief to leave movie world, but a long way back to her student hotel. They offered her a ride in Eric's 2CV to Rue Jacob. She got out. Jean-Claude got out. From there they walked to the Jardin du Luxembourg.

It's a room in a three-star hotel in the seventh *arrondissement*. She is scribbling and waiting for Nash. He has gone out to meet a friend. She has stayed back. She doesn't want to go anywhere. Or see anyone. She's angry that they're in Paris. And irritated that she's with him. She moves from the bed to the window, notebook and pen in hand. Details distinguish the present from the past. They separate what she sees from what she remembers. The women with baguettes and packets tied with string, holding the hands of children, look like the past, but they're the present. They scurry around in the threadbare light. Home to dinner, lovers, *télé*. Whatever people do when they get home.

She isn't home. She's in a hotel room, waiting anxiously to go home although she has just arrived. She inhales and exhales. One and then the other like the pleasure of smoking. On the glass her face stares at her. And beyond is the glare of the Eiffel Tower. She sticks out her tongue and licks the glass. Her saliva on cool glass. Everything appears simple. Even the tower dominating the roofs and trees is simple. The summit lovers hope to reach and never leave. Never leave? Or never reach? An iconic homage to fiction.

Below are streets, parked cars, a café, and blinking lights in the darkness. She thinks it was destiny that brought her back to Paris. She would have never come on her own. Destiny and destination. Two coordinates of fate. She writes it down. *Destiny, what you are helpless not to do. Destination, the place you must do it.* She underlines the words but can't tell if they're profound or fatuous drivel.

When Nash returns, she resumes her place on the bed, scribbling furiously and chewing her lip to signal she still needs to be alone. She doesn't take photos, solely notes to remind her where she has been, what she has seen. She jots down, *Spaniel tied to doorknob.* Trivia drivia.

Behind the bathroom door, he calls. *Sarahhh! O, Sarahhh!* He has a good singing voice, and the syllables tilt like a popular tune. Melismatic.

She remains silent. Begrudgingly silent.

He calls again, water spluttering between the words, echoing against the tiles. Are you getting dressed? The question accented with a splash. We're meeting the Hansons at eight, reservation at nine. Are you dressed?

No! she shrills, meaning she isn't getting dressed. Or meeting Deborah and Steve Hanson. Or going out. Or eating dinner.

Either he has not heard or changed tactics. Solicitous, he asks for her help. Can you get them to send up more towels? Can you do that, darling?

She reaches across the bed for the phone, glancing at the smoke-colored sky. The tower winks at her. Mocking. Lying. Pretending.

2

Nous voulons vivre.
We want to live. – May 1968 graffiti

At nineteen and a recipient of a small grant to study abroad, Sarah left her sheltered life for Paris, carrying a battered suitcase, vestige of her mother's trousseau, and wearing a green wool suit, pencil skirt and boxy jacket. Raised in San Francisco, she'd never been east of Denver. Significant life events numbered four or five: the death of a grandmother, the unrequited love of a high school youth, a broken collarbone, emergency appendicitis, and a bike tour with her brother along the Mendocino coast.

As the plane lifted, she had the sensation of tumbling off a cliff. My God, she muttered, I'm going to a foreign country. I'm going across an ocean. Going, going, going, gone! Competing with the excitement was the itchy discomfort of her stockings. In other words, she'd dressed up for the occasion, assuming that's what girls with grants did. But by the time she arrived in New York, she'd dumped some of her assumptions and put her stockings in a trash bin.

After the plane landed at Orly, she followed the other passengers in puppy fashion from customs to baggage claim through the exit doors to a bus stop where en masse they boarded a bus to Paris. Her first impressions were blurs: small dingy buildings, cafés and Tabacs, canals, and housing projects. Nothing magnificent until they entered the city's center where the bridges and palaces, the river and Eiffel Tower made her dizzy with their magnificence.

At Les Invalides she made her way through the crowded vaulted hall, dragging her heavy suitcase, looking for help. She didn't dare speak French. Or English. She bought several *jetons* and called a few recommended cheap hotels. *Occupé*, she was told over and over. *Occupé. Occupé. Occupé.*

At the Alliance Française they spoke fluent English. The receptionist was helpful and apologetic. Their list of local hotels was available to students enrolled in the school. *Officially enrolled*, she said. She couldn't possibly give Sarah the name from the recommended list. Instead, Sarah would have to come to the premises, take an entrance exam, and pay the fees. Sarah tried to explain that she'd been traveling for twenty-four hours and was beat.

But the receptionist was unrelenting.

She checked her suitcase and timidly set forth, repeating aloud, *Boulevard Raspail, Boulevard Raspail.* The ease of the Metro reassured her. She had come this far. She could go farther. Bearing the signs of a long journey, wrinkled and clammy, she reached the admissions office in late afternoon. She completed the exam. She waited for the evaluation. She paid the fees. She received an official student card with her photo ID. Only to be told the housing office was closed. She would have to return in the morning for a list of hotels.

3

The reflection of Nash's face behind hers is suspended in the window. Glazed and pink. He fondles the top of her head. And smiles. She smiles back. She likes his face: the flat mannish nose, the lively eyes that squint, the gap tooth, the dimple in his right cheek. He radiates confidence. Confident and capable, he negotiates reality.

When Sarah was young and lived in Paris, she learned to skate at the perimeter of reality. When she returned to California, she embraced an uncomplicated existence. A cottage in the Berkeley hills, a kitchen garden, a devotee of Julia Child to the delight of her friends and students, a boyfriend now and then, and the whim of a silk shirt, soft leather shoes, expensive linens. Occupied with teaching, research, and writing, she was grateful to the economic surplus of late twentieth-century America, feminism, and a post in the academy.

Sarah is in her own world, friends complained or admired. *She lives in a dream.*

Nice shower? she asks the window.

Better than Fiesole, worse than Venice.

Nash makes conclusions easily. Opposite from her laborious digressions. Whatever he can touch is reality, which includes her. He makes Sarah feel more substantial than she's able to feel on her own.

Write the Michelin appendix on bathrooms, she suggests.

He laughs. Yes, he should do that.

Nash is a litigator, a sailor and an outdoors man, an invitee to the city's galas, married once when his college girlfriend thought she was pregnant, and once again to VP of Marketing at Nordstrom's. In between he dated pretty salesgirls from shops on Union Street or droll waitresses at the best restaurants. When he met Sarah, he was ready to find a mature woman, meaning a little older and more serious than the usual. If embarrassed by his contentment, even the divorces that failed to cut him down, he inflated his suffering by citing his distant father, cold mother, a girlfriend's abortion, his brother's depression, and looked to Sarah for approval. He considered her an authority on pain. She told him to read poetry.

The poets are the authorities, she said.

Nash's friends were impressed. Sarah Munroe is the best thing that ever happened to you, they said. She'll make you smarter, they teased. As a cum laude graduate of Stanford, he resented the insinuations.

Hers were bewildered, used to seeing her with brainy, unreliable men like Sebastián, her longest relationship. Sarah's type was soulful but nearly broken. She had a knack for attracting them. Those she didn't meet, she could identify on the street or bus or at a party. She never failed to recognize them, and they recognized her, too. When she met Sebastián, a Chilean exile, he went home with her and didn't leave for four years. He couldn't manage anything. Not a job, a car, a cat. He blamed Pinochet.

Nash fingers her wild hair. In their blended reflection, she looks tucked inside him like an origami dove.

We better get going, he says.

I don't think so.

Wear the dress we got in Venice, he says. A hint of how much he loves to spoil her.

I've come down with something.

He touches her forehead and unlatches the window, opening it wide.

Food will cheer you up, he's coaxing, and tomorrow when we're rested, we'll run off to the Louvre. Or wherever you want to go. The Cluny, we'll go there.

He towels the shaving cream off his ears, pulls his socks over the burl of his calves, and swings a damp towel across his loafers.

Bath, shave, clean shirt, I'm a happy guy.

You're so easily pleased, she says.

It's you who pleases me.

More than your Armani shirt?

They laugh in spite of her mood. More than anything, he says ardently.

Then he should understand, shouldn't he? If he's so goddamn fond of her, he should understand.

You meet the Hansons without me, she says.

You'll feel better after I drag you out of this room.

No, she says. Resolute. Her back to him and the dazzling tower. Tell them I'm sick. Tell them I'm sorry I can't come.

4

Le droit de vivre ne se mendie pas, il se prend.
Don't beg for the right to live. Take it. – May 1968 graffiti

In front of the cafeteria at the Alliance Française were two French boys, loitering, no doubt there to pick up foreign girls. Dressed in stiff new jeans, white leather sneakers, and identical sweatshirts printed with a single baffling English word: UNIVERSITY. They noticed her distress and approached her. In clumsy English they conveyed their concern, offering to retrieve her suitcase and drive her to a hotel. Her saviors!

Polite young men, they took her to Les Invalides for her things and delivered her to a cheap hotel. They explained Sarah's predicament to the concierge, a disagreeable old woman, who announced that she intended to call Interpol. Interpol had recently made sensational headlines about white-slave trading after they rescued two Danish girls injected with drugs while trying on lingerie in a shop on the Champs-Élysées. The boys argued that they were not kidnappers. And that their *amie* had nowhere to go. Sarah didn't utter a word.

The concierge held her passport to a lightbulb, grumbled about counterfeits, and handed over the key to a shabby cubicle on the top story of a student hotel, fifth *arrondissement*. A narrow bed, a sooty curtain over the window and inches away, a brick wall.

Sarah collapsed on top of the coverlet, her unopened suitcase beside her on the floor. She slept twelve hours, then rose and rinsed at the sink, changed her clothes, and peered down the charmless hall. She took the small lift to the lobby. The door opened on the world of Paris that lay beyond. However, it was too soon to venture far. She retreated back to the lift now joined by a slim brown man.

Where you from, American girl? She was trained to answer questions without guile. Where you going, American girl?

She innocently told him her room number. He left her on the third floor, but minutes later she heard a knock. It was the same man outside her door, shuffling his feet and gazing at the ground. *Frree-eee lovvv!* he said. She shooed him away like a dog.

On Boul'Mich she encountered dozens of his lonely brethren from the Maghreb, roaming the Latin Quarter, trailing females in short skirts and tight jeans, mumbling words that Sarah first mistook for religious chants. She learned to walk fast and on no account, speak or stop or look them in the eye. Others also frightened her. A young man on a high pediment, pissing on the crowd a death drop below, yelling, *Provo! Provo! Provo!* Another in a basement telephone booth, masturbating while he spoke into the receiver as she watched him from a café table. An old woman who slapped her hand when she couldn't understand French. Another masturbator in the alcove of a building.

After classes she wandered the Left Bank, the boulevards and mazes of small streets. Or crossed the river to check for mail at American Express. There were a few weeks when a young man's schedule synched with hers. The same Metro station at the same time. She soon made a point of searching for him. And pretending he was a friend. Or lover. *Her* French lover. These sightings became the highlight of the day. But he never noticed her, engrossed in a book or intently writing. When he didn't appear, she believed he'd come the next day. Or the next. When days passed without him, she cried. She'd let herself believe he cared about her, too.

5

Sarah has been in the tub for hours. And she's feeling better. After midnight an exuberant Nash crashes through the bathroom door. He kneels on the tile and drums her breastbone with his thumb. *Sarahhh, Sarahhh, Sarahhh,* he croons, while reciting the entire menu. What he ate, what Deborah Hanson ate, what Steve Hanson ate plus the friends they'd brought along.

Repas blanc, he says. White clams, white beans, white veal, white sauce, white bread, white wine, white cake.

Then staggering to the mirror, he lifts an eyelid, pushes out his lips, and rubs a groove of wrinkles by his mouth.

I used to be handsome, didn't I?

Very handsome.

And now?

And now you're. . . .

Don't be cruel to a heart that's true, which he also croons.

Where was the restaurant?

Contrescarpe! Didn't you live there? Steve's friends invited us to visit them in Santa Fe next time we're in the neighborhood.

Nash loves meeting new people. He keeps his calendar booked.

I don't mind missing a good time, she says, trying not to sound testy.

Are you *really* sick? His words trickle into the sink.

Frowning and closing her eyes. I have a bad headache.

Me, too, a zinger from drinking too much Calvados. Contrescarpe! Calvados! Contrescarpe! Contrescarpe! *Calva-uno, dos, tres!*

He stumbles into the bedroom, flicks on the *télé,* and throws himself on the bed.

When he's sober, he'll come to think that the distance between them is his fault. Even her bad mood, his fault. Everything will be put right after he apologizes. A small concession to the last days of their vacation. In the morning he'll tell her he's sorry.

6

Plus je fais l'amour, plus j'ai envie de faire la révolution.
Plus je fais la révolution, plus j'ai envie de faire l'amour.

The more I make love, the more I want to make revolution.
The more I make revolution, the more I want to make love.
— May 1968 graffiti

The mild weather held. Days under milky blue skies, nights shining with stars. In the evenings Sarah followed the streets to the Seine. She walked on the *quais* listening to love murmurs and love grunts. Pressed against the walls, wrapped in each other's coats, a single form made from two. She watched and listened, growing more lonely and more expectant, waiting for him, smelling him, wanting to shout his name.

Three months passed before she met Jean-Claude. The shaggy hair, the long sideburns, the owlish eyes, the lovely slope of nose, they were familiar. Sarah had memorized them on the Metro from *Odéon* to *Opéra*. And then they both responded to a call for extras where Jean-Claude's cousin was an assistant to the film's director.

An hour after the shoot on a bench in the Jardin du Luxembourg, he asked, Why don't you move in with me?

More convenient, she agreed.

And cheaper.

And more amusing.

Unless you find you hate me, he said, tenderly kissing her face, her shoulders, her neck.

I promise to hate you forever.

End of discussion. They scraped together francs for a taxi to transport her things to his *chambre de bonne*. A seventh floor walk-up to what was once a maid's room for the lower apartments of the *grande bourgeoisie*. By the fourth spiral of stairs, they could barely lift the suitcase. They pushed and tugged, and convulsing with laughter fell happily through the door into the tiny room. A kerosene camp stove and cold-water sink made the kitchenette. A wooden box sufficed for a pantry: coffee, sugar, salt, bread, eggs, jam. A sagging bed, a cracked armoire, a broken chair, two hooks and six hangars, crates crammed with books and records. Down the hall a Turkish toilet with two porcelain slabs and a hole in the floor. Actual bathing took place a few blocks away at a public bath with private cubicles for couples. Heat was a small electric unit that worked like a match, making the temperature rise for a moment, then instantly fall. The single window framed the sky and a corner of a building. Crowded under the eaves were doves and on the other side of the alley, a playground where they often heard children.

Above the streets of Paris, they were free to eat when they were hungry, sleep when they were tired, make love whenever they wanted. They were together and didn't question it. And since they couldn't fully speak each other's language, they drew pictures. They signed. Misunderstandings were a problem of language: the wrong assumption or a mistranslation. For necessities there was his university stipend, her grant and father's pension. Coffee, cigarettes, cinema, priority depending on the time of day. They went to a film almost every night. The latest Godard. Imports from Africa, India, Japan. The double features at la Cinémathèque. Avoiding the bright boulevards, they walked through the narrow dark streets past the shuttered shops, the silent churches, the parks to their room. *Theirs.*

As the world burst apart, they said it couldn't affect their love. Whatever happened wouldn't alter their feelings. No matter what, they were together. Always and forever, they said. *Toujours et pour toujours.*

7

In the morning it's Sarah who apologizes. I've been a bad companion, she says. I can't explain why, but it isn't fair. I'm sorry.

Nash suggests a plan. A bite to eat, a walk by the river. No art, no shopping. It's a beautiful day. But she prefers to rest in bed. There is nothing she wants to do. Nowhere she wants to go.

He's trying to be patient but. . . .

Why the hell did we come to Paris?

It was you! I was trying to please you!

You cook French food and buy French clothes and write about French poetry. We came because I thought. . . .

I wish we could go home, she whimpers.

Holding out her arms, he lets them fold around him, hearing her say again that she's sorry. Mutual comfort runs through them, the holding, the closeness. She remembers making love in Venice while canal sounds drifted in and out, rising and sinking until their twin heaviness burst.

He throws the covers to the floor, and pulling on her gown, he rolls over her thigh to enter her.

Nash! I didn't mean . . . .

I guess I'd hoped, he says, adjusting his pants and grabbing his wallet.

As soon as his footsteps fade, Sarah gets out of bed. She stands by the window, watching pedestrians maneuver through the city's commotion. Nash is out there, too, maneuvering among them with his camera and newspaper.

The topaz struts of the tower glitter. A sharp whistle jolts the atmosphere. A bird calls out, and she hums an old tune, "Corrina, Corrina." Jean-Claude used to call her his *petit oiseau* and ask her to sing to him.

I got a bird that whistles
I got a bird that sings

I got a bird that whistles
I got a bird that sings
But if I ain' a-got my Sarah
Life don't mean a thing

8

Oubliez tout ce que vous avez appris. Commencez par rêver.
Forget whatever you've been taught. Start by dreaming.
                    – May 1968 graffiti

The weather turned frosty and gray. Trees dropped their leaves. Fields lay covered in frost. On farms and in villages, people and animals burrowed inside. But in Paris living continued feverishly. Talk was incessant, frenzied, high. Everywhere young people talked and imagined. Their ideas etched with Marx, Trotsky, Bakunin, Fanon, Mao, Situationists, pacifists. Friends or foes? Armed struggle or passive resistance? Force of numbers or guerilla attacks? Sabotage (the word originating from the workers' wooden clogs) versus endangerment to life? Old rivalries flared among ideologies. And visions of student-operated schools, worker-operated factories, and black flags and red flying from rooftops of palaces, churches, ministries. Arguments, discussions, experiments, plots.

Jean-Claude grew up near Lyon. His family were Communists, strict and doctrinaire, one generation out of the confines of the Church into the confines of the Party. Despite superior marks it was unlikely he would find his way to a university. Higher education was tacitly reserved for the middle and upper classes, who recycled their offspring into their own professions of lawyer, financier, doctor, factory owner, and engineer. The new generation of students imagined otherwise. Universities would be classless and open to all.

The Sorbonne's Nanterre annex, a few kilometers north of Paris, was built to decentralize the concentration of young people in the Latin Quarter. Bleak and isolated, it was the perfect replica of class division. When Nanterre students united to protest the Vietnam War, Jean-Claude spoke out. He articulated the students' bond with the underdog, local and international. He himself was France's homegrown version of underdog.

Sarah was an outsider, Jean-Claude's girlfriend from enemy territory. Why should she be blamed for her imperialist forefathers? Why should we? he argued. And sweeping her into his arms, he said, I have sworn to commit my life to Love and Revolution. We are lovers of revolution. And revolutionary lovers.

L'amour, la justice, la liberté pour tous!

La mort aux oppresseurs!

L'amour! La mort! L'amour! La mort!

Sarah heard no distinction. And it scared her. Love and death, to her ears they sounded the same.

9

Normal is what Sarah loves about Nash. Not boring but consistent. He makes plans and follows through. He arrives on time. He likes sports but doesn't obsess over losing. He cries at sentimental movies. He enjoys holidays. His favorite food is pizza. He's an enthusiast who appreciates ordinary pleasures.

After they met, he enticed her to join him sailing in the Bay and hiking on Mount Tam. She has become a hiker and a sailor. The intoxicating air, the wild waves, the forests, the bald California hills, they strip away all pretension. They've given her another perspective. Pantheistic, she might gleefully say. And it's Nash who initiated this transformation in her.

Nash has heard about her year in Paris and her radical French boyfriend. The exhilarating days and embattled nights of *soixante-huit*. The takeover of the streets. The brutality of the police. The closure of every French institution.

He compares her 1968 to his own. He was active in campus protests. He burned his draft card and lived in a commune. He was arrested for vandalizing a weapons lab. But despite clashes with police, teargas, and a few days in jail, his experiences weren't visceral. Rather, exercises of intellect and empathy. And after the war ended and his career had begun, he placed those events in the chronology of a colorful and rebellious past.

With Sarah it's different. She speaks of those times with great passion. Paris is a city for the living, and it's there where I first came alive, she tells him. She doesn't mention the part of her that died.

When Nash asked about her wedding band, she lied. She said it was an heirloom. Anyway it couldn't be called a wedding. More like a scene from "theater of the absurd." A pagan ritual for a clan of tree nymphs. Forbidden to any church and all states. The bride in a satin slip, a woolen shawl, galoshes, and a chain of withered weeds around her neck, and the groom in a moth-eaten cutaway and top hat. On a drizzly winter solstice, friends drove them to a field near Fontainebleau. They waded across a stream into the woods, Eric on flute playing Albinoni's Adagio in G minor and Jean-Claude reciting Breton's "L'Union libre," *Ma femme aux doigts de hasard et d'as de coeur.* They pronounced themselves a union. Later on Place de la Contrescarpe, he slipped a gold band on Sarah's finger. Ceremony and ring were never mentioned again.

By March Jean-Claude was occupied at school, not by academics but tactics and manifestos. Meetings all day and night, meaning he rarely came home. Or when he was there, he was tired and agitated. He criticized Sarah. He said her opinions were naive and uninformed. Not serious enough, he accused. Too much of a free spirit. *Free union*, yes. *Free spirit*, no. It was difficult for her to understand the difference. She thought *free spirit* was what everyone aspired to be.

She dropped out of school to work as an artist's model. She accepted a gig with Shelley Bell, a rambunctious Englishman and successful painter. He'd lived in Paris for twenty years and claimed a pedigree from his namesake Percy Bysshe. A legend in my own time, he said. His ramblings punctuated with lecherous jokes and lewd looks. Nonetheless, she agreed to let him paint her.

Shelley Bell's studio was a small house on the outskirt of the city. Its walls filled with drawings and paintings in charcoal, pen, acrylic, and oil. All of them of breasts and buttocks in bright, blunt colors. Nothing subtle. As Sarah undressed, he chatted, laughed at his own jokes, readied his palette and brushes, and went to work. For hours a trance overtook him. He didn't utter a word. But after the session was over and Sarah was dressed, the bawdy palaver resumed. He promised to make her famous as his muse. He even asked her to marry him.

Nash has seen photos of Sarah when she lived in Paris. Beautiful, young Sarah. Her long honey-colored hair piled on her head, her dark unplucked brows, her sad hazel eyes, her violet lips, tall and willowy in tight jeans and tight fuzzy sweaters.

Can you call the bookstore? he asks, meaning Shakespeare and Company where Shelley used to hold court. If possible, Nash wants to buy a painting of her.

She agrees to call. The clerk has Shelley's number. He answers, and Sarah tells him who she is. It takes a few seconds before there is friendly recognition and his Dionysian laugh.

Sarah, you've come back to me! I knew someday you'd come!

She hands Nash the receiver.

This is Sarah's fiancé, he says. She's not feeling well, but while we're here, I'd like to meet you and see any work of Sarah.

The *Sarah Series* sold years ago, he says, but he promises to dig up a sketch or two. They make an appointment to meet the next day.

Sarah hasn't left the hotel. She hasn't gotten dressed. She eats what Nash brings back to the room. While he's out, she watches the street or lies in bed, thinking of Jean-Claude.

Are you sure you won't come with me? He's off to Giverny.

Tomorrow, she promises. Tomorrow, I'll come with you.

10

Embrasse ton amour sans lâcher ton fusil.
Embrace your love without dropping your gun. – May 1968 graffiti

In the alcove by the stairs, Jean-Claude rigged a lockbox. In it were talc, sugar, baking soda, and chalk plus oversized leather-bound books that he bought from the *bouquinistes* along the Seine. The books were in Greek, German, Arabic, and Chinese. When Sarah asked what he wanted with them, he said it wasn't any of her business. When their room reeked of vinegar and ammonia and she asked again, he told her to stop pestering him. When she found him cutting hollows in the center of the books, she wondered why.

To hide things, he said.

Hide what? We own nothing.

My *dernier recours* goes into the book.

Last resort of what?

Arrête! With the questions every minute!

He was constantly away, and Sarah seldom went with him. She was working to pay for rent and food. When he was home, he was exhausted. When he was awake, they talked a little, smoked, and waited. Looking out the window at the sky, it seemed they were always waiting. Jean-Claude waiting to leave. Sarah waiting for him to return.

11

Last winter Nash was seized by the notion of a romantic voyage: Italy, Portugal, France. Anything strike your fancy? he asked Sarah.

Anywhere, she said absently. She was busy teaching and writing with a deadline for a publication. Wherever you want to go is fine as long as you work out the itinerary.

She sits in the back of the plane. Away from him, no distractions. She tells him she needs to grade papers. She wishes she hadn't agreed to come. She's angry she'd been accommodating. Accommodating, that's her weakness.

Beside her a friendly passenger clutches miniature bottles of vodka, laughing and lifting her hands. She begins to chat as soon as Sarah sits down. Laugh and chat. A sane, friendly laugh. She orders Bloody Mary mix for both of them. After she and Sarah are settled with their drinks, she begins:

I lived in Los Angeles for twenty-five years, married to a French professor. When he accepted a position to host a group of students abroad, we moved to Grenoble. Our two children and five others under our care. The father of my favorite often wrote to me to check on his daughter. He sent me notes of gratitude and a gift for Christmas. Polite notes that became personal. He confided in me about his unhappy marriage, and I confided about mine. We began to write more often. Daily. After a year my family made plans to go back to California. He suggested I stop in Boston to meet him. I lied and told my husband I was visiting a college friend. We arranged a date in the atrium of the Gardner Museum. When I arrived, I was shaking like a virgin. We held each other for many minutes. He said, You're just as I imagined. *Which amused me since I'm not much for the imagination. At least, not a young woman by thirty years. But he loved me. I knew there would be recriminations, resentment, confusion, maybe hate. But I never went home again.*

12

Ici, bientôt, de charmantes ruines.
Coming soon to this location: charming ruins. – May 1968 graffiti

From Dr. King's funeral in Atlanta, Sarah's cousin wrote, *Azaleas in bloom. April is the cruelest month.* Sarah understood. She no longer found pleasure in the beautiful diversions of Paris. Beauty was a distraction from everything that was wrong.

Jean-Claude asked her to deliver a book. One of the large hollow tomes that he'd wrapped in brown paper. The address was a café off the Champs-Élysées. It was a warm spring day. Tables were assembled on the sidewalks for lunch, the atmosphere festive and forgetful. Everyone looking shamelessly gorgeous.

He instructed her to wait fifteen minutes at one end of the café counter. No longer than twenty. The recipient would identify himself by whistling. If he did not appear, she should drop the book in the garbage.

Sarah stood, her elbows pressed on the package as if it might fly away. Punctually, a well-dressed man with pomaded black hair, deeply lined pale skin, sunglasses, and a trim short beard approached her. The tune he whistled was the theme from Stravinsky's *L'histoire du soldat*. He didn't speak or shake her hand but bowed curtly and held out his palms. She placed the package on them, and he promptly left. She ordered a coffee, trying to stay calm, inspecting the room for a sign that she'd been noticed.

Afterwards, she dashed towards the river, fuming over the stranger, especially his bow, a gesture of ridicule. She was sure that Jean-Claude had used her but unsure how. Unsure if it was wrong to be used. And if their cause required *by any means necessary*. Frightened to let her thoughts run to her complicity in something she knew nothing about.

Her pace slowed as she doubled back across the river into the Marais, passing Jewish shops and unfashionable people, darting like a fugitive beneath shadows, humming *sotto voce* Stravinsky's jaunty refrain. Tragic if you know the tale: a soldier returns from war with his violin. The violin sings, *I'm alive! I'm alive! I survived! I survived!* He plays as he travels home to meet his sweetheart. But instead, he meets the Devil in disguise. A dubious bargain is struck. In exchange for knowledge of the future, he loses what he loves most.

Recently, she'd asked Jean-Claude about their future. *Toujours and pour toujours?* They'd once been his words. But now it was a question she knew better than to ask.

We don't know what's going to happen, he said.

Later, she thought his uncertainty was false. And that he knew but refused to say.

13

After Nash leaves, Sarah props the telephone directory on the bed. It sits beside her like a grenade, inert but possessing deadly potential. She taps the cover, tapping lightly, then frantically until she musters the courage to open it. She thumbs her way to L. Le. Lec. Leclerc. There are columns of listings. She lifts the receiver. She dials the first Leclerc Jean-Claude. Busy. Busy again. Wrapping a raincoat over her nightgown, she runs downstairs to the street into a warm drizzle. The tower hovers in the clouds. Like a god it is everywhere.

In the doorway of the café is a party of men, tan and middle-aged, accompanied by two voluptuous girls, too young to be with older men. All of them tipsy and loud as if they've come from an all-night party. The men swagger around, pawing the girls, pulling their hair, tweaking their ass, rubbing up against them, and laughing loudly. Sarah watches, their sensuality stirring regret, judgment, aversion, desire.

One of the men lobs her a dirty look. *Con*, he mutters.

She gulps her espresso and returns to the hotel, up the stairs and back to bed. The line is no longer busy.

Oui? a man answers.

Excusez-moi but I am looking for Jean-Claude, Jean-Claude Leclerc, she says.

Oui, c'est moi. He swallows. *Et vous?*

Sarah tells him her name. She says she lived in Paris twenty years ago and knew a Jean-Claude Leclerc. Each time the man attempts to speak, she prevents him. The public baths, she says, the blind samurai movies, the Luxembourg Gardens, the field near Fontainebleau, do you remember?

Finally, he is able to interrupt.

I am not this Leclerc, he says.

Mais êtes-vous sûr?

Of course, I'm sure!

C'est un autre, madame, Monsieur Jean-Claude Leclerc repeats, *Je suis désolé, madame.*

A second Leclerc Jean-Claude's line is out-of-order. A third is also busy. She expects to be disappointed. She tries the next listing. It rings five times. An answering machine clicks on the recording: *Jean-Claude Leclerc n'est pas ici.*

She immediately hangs up. She lies back on the pillow, panting. She calls back and listens. And hangs up again. She rests her head on the cradle of the phone, caressing the plastic, her heart pounding in her ears. He's in Paris. They are here together. Under the same sky, the same mocking tower. Anytime she can call the number and hear his voice. She redials and listens to the five rings, waiting for the message: *Jean-Claude Leclerc n'est pas ici.* Not here? Goddamn him. Goddamn him to hell. She hangs up. Again the rings and the voice: *Jean-Claude Leclerc n'est pas ici.* No indication of where he is, no referral number, no information if he's out of town or how he can be reached in case of emergency. Isn't this an emergency?

An hour later Sarah keeps her promise to Nash. She feels better. Almost buoyant. She bathes. She puts on his favorite dress and wears her hair down. She walks briskly to the Musée d'Orsay, the ornate train station converted to a showplace for masterpieces of art.

Nash and Shelley wait at a nearby café. As soon as she passes through the door, Shelley's laugh assails her. The man is unmistakably himself. At least, she can credit him with that. Painting, drinking, carousing have agreed with him because after twenty-five years, he looks well. His unruly hair is thinner, sprinkled with white, and grazes his shoulders. His tobacco-stained teeth are missing a cuspid. His clothes, carelessly worn, are dabbed with paint, and there's an orange Indian scarf and a string of beads around his neck. All in all, well.

Hello, beauty, he says. His small, vivacious eyes leveling at her chest.

Hello, beast. She bends to kiss him. Both cheeks.

He whistles and pinches her bottom.

Rather than taking offense, Sarah hugs him forcefully. He is incontrovertible proof, evidence that she too lived in Paris. Yes, she breathed and ate and slept in Paris. And met and lost her. . . .

She excuses herself from the table. She buys a *jeton* and locates the telephone next to the W.C. She dials Jean-Claude's number. Five rings. *Jean-Claude Leclerc n'est pas ici.* Bastard, liar, deserter, thief!

You okay? Nash asks.

Fine, fine, she says.

Shelley sips a brandy, recounting to Nash the stories of men who'd been in love with Sarah Munroe. Of course, no one could get near her with that militant chap she kept in tow. He tweaks his beard, and his mouth puckers with disdain.

What a gloomy fellow he was. Never a friendly word, never a smile. But we could dream, couldn't we?

You're ridiculous, she says.

But it's true. Whenever she came into the bookstore, they'd huddle. Young, old, deaf, dumb, they were stunned. My poet friend Demetrius had never seen such a face except in statues. *A living face,* he said. He wrote odes about her. One night he read the Prologue to the *Iliad* in ancient Greek while an American *noir* played bass. Remember, Sarah? Of course, you remember. They dedicated the reading to you.

Don't believe any of it!

Another admirer was an Irishman. What was his name, Bertie? Patty? You had to wipe the drool off his dimpled chin. You know how the Irish worship Nature! But that Frenchman of yours. Wasn't he wanted by the police? Wasn't he arrested?

Sarah has heard enough. She can't stand to hear more.

I was coming on fifty when I met her. Shelly slaps Nash's thigh. I'm what you call a specialist. I didn't want to touch. I only wanted to paint.

14

Sous les pavés, la plage.
Under the paving stones, the beach. – May 1968 graffiti

At about 9 pm the first barricades went up spontaneously. Everyone recognized instantly the reality of their desires in that act. – René Viénet

The Mouvement du 22 Mars started at Nanterre as an antiwar demonstration and the occupation of a building. The dozen or so protestors were soon joined by hundreds. And by early May the uprising reached central Paris.

Vite! That was the shout in the streets.

Vite! The signal for revolt.

Vite! When the university was occupied by police.

Vite! When the battle for the Latin Quarter began.

Vite! As hundreds of barricades were built of cobblestones, trees, cement mixers, metal drums, and burning cars.

Vite! When students marched and sang.

Vite! Wrapped in flags, red for communist and black for anarchist.

Vite! When they resisted.

Vite! When they felt the rush of lust.

Vite! When they wrote their ideals on the forbidden walls.

Vite! And fought for freedom with clubs, crowbars, and chains.

Vite! And ran from nightsticks, water cannons, concussion grenades, and teargas.

Vite! When they demanded a new government.

Vite! And a new definition of *liberté, égalité, fraternité.*

Vite! When they were beaten and dragged into police vans. And left their blood on sidewalks and barricades.

Paris erupted. A million marched, waving white handkerchiefs, *Adieu, de Gaulle! Adieu!*

Ten million workers went on strike. Executives went on strike.

The Metro and buses stopped.

Newspapers, municipal services, and trains stopped.

Schools, banks, markets, harbors, and airports shut down.

From city to city and town to town, the streets were liberated. France was closed.

On the last day of May almost a million loyalists staged a countermarch in support of de Gaulle. By early June the unions began to sell out their workers. Those resistant were pressured, bribed, threatened to return to factories.

I can't stay, Jean-Claude told Sarah.

But what if? Trying to hold on.

I must go, or there won't be time to get out.

I'll come with you.

That's no good.

But I can . . . please, please, she said.

Two can't run. Two can't hide.

Jean-Claude didn't say *au revoir*, meaning "see you again." He said, *Adieu* as if he were leaving forever.

15

For their last day Nash suggests a ride on a *bateau-mouche*. Scenic and relaxing, he says persuasively. Sarah is used to his persuasions. For the trip she had left all the decisions to him. At the time she assumed she could look at Paris with a new man in a mature way. But hearing the same sounds, seeing the same streets, meeting Shelley, the veil of memories has lifted. And engulfed her. Sarah is barely above water. Barely breathing.

16

La barricade ferme la rue mais ouvre la voie.
Barricades close the streets but open the way. – May 1968 graffiti

On June 6, 1968, the day of Robert Kennedy's assassination, Sarah flew home to San Francisco. For weeks she lay around. Listless and anxious, unable to rid herself from the shame and terror of her last days in Paris. In September she moved to Berkeley. She resumed her studies, took on extra assignments, and worked part-time as a translator. She joined the antiwar movement, and at the battle for People's Park, exactly a year after the uprising in Paris, it was déjà vu: an armed military camp, bayonets and teargas, street violence, huge marches, the murder of James Rector and blinding of Alan Blanchard, followed by community outrage and school closures.

A letter eventually arrived at her mother's house in Noe Valley.

This came for you, she said.

An Italian postmark and Italian stamp with SARAH MUNROE printed in block letters and no return address. For a year she'd been waiting for Jean-Claude to make contact, waiting for them to begin again. Across a sheet of tissue-thin paper was a fishing pole with a line dangling a worm. Below the worm he'd written in English, *Alive under the ground* and a single word in French, *Oublie.*

Forget? she cried. How am I supposed to forget?

Under a fiery night sky, she dreams of a countless number of people. Swarming around and shouting. She shouts, too. Her throat aches from shouting. In her sleep like a voice-over, she hears the chant.

Vite! Vite! Vite! Vite!

She reaches out to take Jean-Claude's hand as his face swells into a giant balloon, rising and floating out of sight.

Years later *Time* featured an article about radicals of the era, including Jean-Claude Leclerc's emergence from the underground. In the magazine his hair is dark and neatly parted, his chin bearded and cheeks gaunt, his shoulders stooped. He's wearing a black leather jacket and black shirt. He peers at the camera over his glasses and smiles. A smile that makes Sarah cry.

AFTER HIDING IN ITALY FOR SEVENTEEN YEARS, TEACHING KINDERGARTEN, LECLERC WAS ASKED WHAT HE INTENDED TO DO IF CLEARED OF CONSPIRACY CHARGES IN FRANCE. "ORGANIZE!" HE RETORTED.

She showed the article to Nash. He was my boyfriend, she said proudly.

For a minute we took up the burdens of the world, Nash said. When we tired of that, we took up the burden of ourselves.

She disagreed. It was more than an exercise of the moment. It was a real revolution. It was meant to make real change.

And did it?

Yes, some things changed.

Two steps forward, one step back.

17

The river, the *quais*, the bridges, the parks explode under the soft gray sky. Sarah closes her eyes, inhaling the city. The boat ride is enough Paris for her. She tells Nash she wants to go back to the hotel. She falls on the bed, her sanctuary, while he flicks on the TV. It's the French Open. The tournament has been ongoing since they arrived. Whenever he's in the room, the *télé* is on. The thwack of the ball, the alternating hush and roar of the crowd, the concentrated faces of opponents torment her. She has come to hate tennis.

Want me to undress you?

No, I have a chill.

Want me to cover you up?

Not that either. Sarah only wants him to leave her alone. But doesn't know how to tell him that he can never compete with a phantom lover. But if she doesn't tell him, how is he supposed to understand? Tears flood her face. She drifts to sleep and sees a deep blue dome with a thousand kites in flight over the Tuileries. She's running in her old heather-green wool suit. It looks better than she remembers. Above the river is Jean-Claude, again so large that his legs straddle the Seine. He's waving *Le Figaro*, May 1968. She can see a picture of them. It covers the entire page.

You look happy! he shouts at her.

People don't make other people happy! she shouts back.

Then she starts to sob. But you did, you did, you did!

Nash is calling her through the noise of the TV. She is being called out of sleep. She doesn't want to wake up before she tells Jean-Claude something urgent. But now she isn't going to remember. Nash is calling her back.

You were sobbing, he says, kissing her. You were sobbing in your sleep.

It takes courage to love, as much courage as it takes to fight, that's what she wanted to tell him.

Hush, he says, it was just a sad dream.

He puts his arms around her. He is tender, and she is grateful. That's the best they can manage. He says if she's well enough to venture out, she should choose a restaurant.

Our first and last dinner in Paris together, he says wistfully.

I can do that, she says.

He suggests looking in Michelin. But since she is choosing, he'll have to submit to her method: walk in the direction of Saint-Germain-des-Prés and randomly find a quiet side street.

Fuck Michelin! they laugh.

It's eight o'clock when they leave the hotel. A balmy night, everyone is on the street. On Rue du Dragon she points, There! She seats herself at an outdoor table with a checkered cloth and candles under a festoon of white lights and pots of red geraniums.

Nash frowns. No one else is here, he says, trying to sound neutral.

It's cheerful, she says. I like that.

Okay, he says. He's going to be a good sport. I think I'll risk a steak.

Living dangerously?

Don't be nasty.

You're the one who said it was a risk.

I thought they might try to slip me horse.

Get the steak, I'll get the mussels.

He takes her hand. You've been so moody here, he says.

The pressure between their fingers is cool and insubstantial. Two shadows trying to connect.

Want to come back next year?

I never want to come back, surprised at how spiteful she sounds, sensing she might start to cry if she has to speak about loving and hating Paris.

Fortunately, the food is very tasty. Nash says it's the best meal he has had on the trip.

The traffic dwindles. There's a glamorous woman with a wolfhound. And a moment later, two men strolling arm in arm. They stop and change positions, their faces lit. The older man is tall and bald with glasses and a beakish nose. But the other one? He's familiar. Sarah gapes at his face, his hair, his physique. The pair steps back into the shadows, but she can partly see them. It's Jean-Claude's face, Jean-Claude's hair, Jean-Claude's physique. In a city of millions, it's Jean-Claude.

You look as if you've seen a ghost, Nash says.

Sarah says nothing. She studies the pair across the street. The height, the shape of the nose, the color of hair, the slight stoop, the handsome mouth. The anomaly is the white linen suit, fashionably baggy, which shocks her. She would never imagine Jean-Claude in a suit like that.

The two men walk on.

Nash, do you mind? I'll be right back, she cries.

Before he can say a word, she runs into the street. At Saint-Germain the crowd thickens. She trails the back of the white linen suit. She passes them, trotting to the end of the block so she can turn in their direction. They continue their stroll, pausing at shop windows where Jean-Claude is blocked. They start to move forward, their faces in full view. His face is identical to the one she remembers, but it's the face of a youth. A twenty-year old. Another Jean-Claude.

18

On achète ton bonheur. Vole-le.

You're already buying happiness. Steal it. – May 1968 graffiti

A t the corner there's a telephone booth. Five rings and the message. *Jean-Claude Leclerc n'est pas ici.* She waits for the message tone and begins.

Jean-Claude, her voice quakes. This is your old friend, Sarah Mun . . .

Several crackles on the line. Sarah! Sarah Munroe!

Jean-Claude, are you there? She's confused.

Of course, I'm here! he shouts excitedly. You called me!

I'm sorry, but you startled me. I didn't think you were in town.

Where are you?

I'm here, too.

He's confused. You're here in Paris? And you haven't called?

I've called a dozen times. But you were never home.

Maybe I run out for a coffee or baguette, but I haven't left the house in weeks.

Are you all right?

Of course not! he laughs.

He asks how she is, and she tells him she was sick. But I'm better now, she says. I'm leaving soon.

Not too soon, he protests.

She explains that she was calling to hear his voice on the recording. I'm happy to know you're alive, she says.

Sarah, he whispers. Sarah, Sarah, I was thinking of you today. About you and the Fates.

I try to forget about them, she says.

He chuckles harshly. You can forget them, but they never forget you. They're always with us, threading and spinning their blows. And that's why I thought of you.

She doesn't believe him.

And out of the blue, you called.

He asks if she received his letter. He asks if she knew he was on the run for many years.

But it's too much to explain over the phone, he says.

She understands. He wants her to come to him. After all these years, come to him.

Where are you?

Near Saint-Germain.

I'm not far. It would be nice to get out of my apartment.

I don't think so.

But you called?

Only to hear your voice.

Ah, the recording is better than the man? Representation *préférable* to reality? he laughs again.

She understands the allusion to Guy Debord. Debord was one of his mentors.

When I hear your voice, I can see you clearly, she says.

But you don't really want to see me?

I've been upset.

And if you see me, it will upset you more.

Yes. Probably.

At least, tell me something about your life. Didn't we once tell each other everything?

A primitive hurt churns inside her. You didn't, she says.

But I wanted to. Please don't doubt I wanted to.

Doubting has become my nature.

Mine, too.

I couldn't tell you or it might have . . . compromised your safety. I wanted to protect you.

I wanted to be as brave as you.

Be brave now, Sarah. Come and see me.

I can't. My fiancé is waiting.

And he's the jealous type?

I'm leaving him, she says.
And after will you come?
I'm hanging up, Jean-Claude.
But then will you?
Adieu!

19

Sarah walks past the pair of men again. Arm in arm. One is tall and bird-like, and the other? A beautiful, young twin of Jean-Claude. She herself feels beautiful and strong. She walks without stopping, tossing her hair like a mane, directly to the hotel and up the four flights of stairs to the room. She leaves the new luggage, the new raincoat from Florence, the skimpy dress Nash bought her in Venice. The atmosphere is warm but no longer bright. Thick clouds rumble through the sky. And beneath the clouds, the glorious tower is smiling at her, smiling like something animate and alive. She puts what she needs in a shopping bag. It isn't much. She has never needed much. She thinks that she had better write Nash a note. Better to finish it off right. Isn't that what she'd been struggling to do? Struggling so much it made her sick.

Dear Nash. My dearest Nash. My dear friend Nash. She wants to wish him great happiness. A wonderful life. And to thank him.

She picks up her bag and walks into the night towards Boulevard des Invalides.

A Love Story No, War

We need, in love, to practice only this: letting each other go.
For holding on comes easily; we do not need to learn it.

—Rainer Maria Rilke, "Requiem for a Friend"

Part 1

It was your idea to go away, and I agreed. Mostly to please you. These days I'm not so good at pleasing you. I don't feel it's required, but sometimes it's part of the compromise we've agreed to. Anyway you said we'd visit Valley of the Moon, and who can resist the sound of that? It's the place Jack and Charmian London loved, and you said you'd like to see the ruins of their estate.

I didn't want to go away. I never do. I like to stay home, and you like to travel. However, if you can pry me, I'm enthralled. Even driving on California freeways fills me with wonder. Like how did we ever come to this?

Unfortunately, when you're driving, I don't get to daydream much. I'm too concerned. You speed and weave and cut off monster trucks. I'm certain you're going to have an accident. I guess it has to do with the breakdown of trust between us. I remember when we first met, I said what a wonderful driver you were. It was when you smoked, and the Camels, the superb Peugeot, the way you gripped the wheel impressed me. Smoking, grinning, driving. It was entirely superficial, but that's what impressions are.

I don't think people change. No, not really. Life changes them. Life has changed you. And me. Now we're different, and it's no one's fault. I love you, but you're not the same man so it's logical I don't love you in the same way. It makes you feel bad. Worse, it makes you feel small. That's what I hate. Seeing you small when the memories of your big hands still give me chills.

Valley of the Moon is close so the drive was short. Much of it across the flat, glossy landscape of river delta. Serpentine waterways winding in and out. Plum and almond trees in blossom which aggravated your sinuses. Driving became even more precarious when you blew your nose.

We arrived at our friend's vacant country house in the dark. The blowzy spring day had turned bitter cold. In keeping with your hopeful romantic spirit, you decided to make a fire. The wood was in a shed behind the patio, but the winter had been long and stormy so naturally the wood was wet. You checked the flue, balled up newspaper, laid twigs on top. It was hard to get a fire going. Your attempts soon started to smoke. It wasn't your fault. You know how to make a fire. In fact, you're very skillful in the wild.

I learned that our first year, too. You took us to Idaho and put us in a rubber raft and rowed us down the Middle Fork of the Salmon River. It was marvelous. Almost every moment except the evening before we started off when I heard the river rushing by and feared what would happen once I was rushing with it. We were out eight days, and you cooked beef Stroganoff and pineapple upside-down cake, and maneuvered through the rapids like an otter.

It was terrible how much the fire smoked. I was worried our friend's house would stay smokey for weeks. Although it was cold, we had to open the windows and doors. So much for your fantasy of lying bare bottom on a hearth rug.

For dinner we decided on something simple instead of one of the village's restaurants, over-priced and over-precious. You went down to the corner store and returned with two Idaho potatoes and a head of lettuce.

I turned the electric oven up to 500 degrees, washed the potatoes, and put them in. You rinsed the lettuce and scraped the carrots for a salad. While the potatoes cooked, you sat on the sofa with a book on Afghanistan, part of your obsession with the Middle East and written by a former colleague from grad school. I read a novel by a fashionable New York writer.

Twenty minutes later there was a muffled explosion in the vicinity of the kitchen. You jumped with fright. You're easily startled by unexplained noises, I've never known why. Right away I knew a potato had burst. Not only had half our meager meal disintegrated, but now bits of crusted potato coated the inside of the oven.

The smoke, the weather, the potato, they did not augur well. We ate one potato and went to bed. Strange beds are one reason I don't like to travel. You could say I'm fussy. You say it all the time. I admit it, but how am I to help it? It's a fact, but it shouldn't be a crime. I don't make you feel your nature is a crime. Or do I?

You don't like covers, but I need warmth and weight. You found extra blankets on a shelf in the guest room closet which I piled on my side of the bed. They were heavy like the metal apron a dentist puts over your chest when you have x-rays. You fell asleep right away. You're prone to it. I stayed up reading my disappointing novel until my eyelids drooped. Then I turned off the bedside lamp and went to sleep.

Every morning you used to ask me how I slept. I got tired of the same question, especially listening to myself complain about a bad or restless night. Plus I don't like to talk in the morning. Your question was a habit from your months in Africa. There, people always asked how you slept, how your wife slept, how your children slept, how your parents slept until they had exhausted inquires about everyone in the family. Your question obliged me to ask you in return. Like the question, your answer never varies. You're a great sleeper.

It had been raining off and on for a week. In the morning as I was cleaning potato from the oven, heavy showers returned. I made tea. You made espresso. We returned to our seats by the cold fireplace. Most of the smokey smell was gone. My novel hadn't improved which surprised me. I thought it would get better.

You tried looking cheerful, which in your case is a caricature of cheerfulness. However, it's not a joke. Your depression has permeated your physical being. Your body is muscle fit but tight like a girdle, guarding you from everything. Your intellectual liveliness bound and bunched up. You look angry with an angry brow and angry thin lips and eyes shrunk back in their deep-set sockets. In fact, you look like a potato about to explode.

However, that's the surface. Inside, I know you're lonely. I know you want me to ease the loneliness. I know that's why you insisted we come here. It was supposed to be for me. It was supposed to take me away from my piles of work. But really it's for you. That's why I don't mind so much. And we had a nice lunch in Petaluma. The cream of chard soup was delicious. And they made the most beautiful cakes I've ever seen, small and square and lop-sided like a Thiebaud painting. You liked the walk through town, especially the clock shop. You love clocks. That's why I got you one made from a hubcap. That's why you brought one back from Hong Kong with Mao Zedong waving the Little Red Book as the second-hand.

But things can only please a person for so long. That's the problem with things. They're momentary. You know that, which is why you hardly care about anything anymore.

The rain delayed our excursion to the London estate. Late morning we drove to Valley of the Moon. The sky cleared to milky gray, and white pillows of clouds rolled by.

To Whom It May Concern:

I am pleased to provide this letter of recommendation for Franklin Teller. Franklin Teller was employed at Crown Hollow Software Publications for seven years and provided valuable input on all our published materials. During his stay here, he was able to communicate well with the software engineers and translate their technical concepts into commonplace prose for our customer base.

Crown Hollow was a small company so it was extremely important that staff work well together. Frank's point of view was motivated by a high standard of performance.

I recommend him for employment without qualification. Please do not hesitate to contact me if you need additional information.

Sincerely yours,

Louise B. Henderson
Vice President of Production (former)
Crown Hollow Software Publications
c/o P.O. Box 14654
San Francisco, CA 94112
(415) 872-9560
lbh@earthlink.net

Dear Frankie,

If you want to know the truth, I'll tell you the truth. Always have, always will. You are a great writer. Don't let anyone tell you different. I saved all your letters from camp, starting in 5th grade, HS, college. The best was after you moved to New York. You was flying high then. You was my boy. I've got them arranged by year if you want them, stored in your camp trunk with a couple of mitts and other crap.

I don't know what was wrong with your mother. She thought I was the smartest man she ever met, but I told her you was smarter. And you did so great in school. Hell, I never did great. You were such a goody-goody, too. You'd think she'd appreciate it after what Bruce Weinstein and Harold Betz put their mothers through. As far as I'm concerned, you can take the whole crowd and drive them over a cliff. I'm still mad about them parking on my lawn. Never did think they were up to your level. Didn't they call themselves the Bucks? You thought they were better than sliced bread. Did I ever tell you the day you came home and told me you were a Buck, I barfed!

I heard Bruce died of leukemia. That's a real shame. From time to time I run into Harold. He drives a 190 SL. That was the car your mother wanted me to get back when. She thought I'd look cute in a sports car. She thought I'd look cute with a driving cap on my bald head. That's when Mercedes weren't a dime a dozen. That's because Jews didn't drive German cars. Now every Jew has a Benz or a Beamer.

Do not doubt yourself one minute. Not even a minute is what I say. That's what made me a good salesman. I wasn't capable of self-doubt. Sometimes I get the feeling it's something nasty your mother said to you. You believe in that crap? A little criticism turning a man into a wuss? You're tougher than that.

Maybe it wasn't what she said. Maybe it was that look of hers. Watch out! If I let myself concentrate, I can still see it staring back at me. I bet you see it, too. From the day you was born. I'm not saying she didn't love you. She loved you, she loved you.

The time you won the essay contest for *Teen Times*, she was proud.

She called up everybody she knew. Friends she hadn't seen in ten years. But she was jealous. You know how with a jealous person you can never tell whether you coming or going. They hate you one minute, worship you the next. Maybe she was jealous because her father wanted her to be a writer. Why? Because he tried to be a playwright and ended up selling insurance. You believe in that crap? I guess I've turned into a regular bedside shrink.

YOU are going to get better soon. YOU are going to get back on your feet. YOU are going to write that book you been talking about. Take care, son. I'll call you Sunday.

Love, *Dad*

Jess stopped by last night. Did you tell her you'd be home? I told her you're at group therapy every Tuesday night. She said she didn't know. She asked me, What's going to happen to Frankie? I hate when they call you *Frankie*. I hate baby names. They don't even sound endearing. I was civil. I sat her down and made chamomile tea. Her questions are endless. She's the kind of person who asks questions instead of making conversation. I told her to write them down so you can call her tomorrow and answer yourself. I'm too tired to remember.

From Jess:

1. Do you remember IF mom visited me in college? I'm blanking. Gail swore she met mother once. She can even remember what mom wore. I think she's confused with the time we all got together in New York. What do you think?

2. Is therapy working?

3. Do you want to drive down with me for Dad's birthday?

4. Can you stay with Stella one night next week so I don't go stark raving mad?

Hey, I'm not the one who should be complaining. Right?

Love ya, Jess

sorry to rush off
appt at 7:30
how was therapy?

take dry cleaning
spot on brown collar
SHOW them
(if you don't show they won't see)

ALSO can you weed
if you don't feel like it
hire worker on 4th
don't let them charge < $10/hr

ONE more thing
if you make date w/Jess
do it at her house OK?
out the door -- L

JOB DESCRIPTION

Posting Title:	Writing Program Coordinator
Requisition:	002372
Department:	Student Learning Center
Location:	Main Campus
Salary:	$42,500 - $59,000 Annually

This requisition will remain open until filled.

Job Description:

The University of California seeks an experienced, energetic, and visionary professional to coordinate its writing program.

Responsibilities:

The position entails addressing the diverse academic writing needs of students as they transition into the University and across academic disciplines. The incumbent must have specific knowledge of and experience working with immigrant students, English second language learners and first generation students. The writing coordinator is responsible for managing, designing and implementing an effective tutorial program; supervising 60+ undergraduate and graduate tutors; developing a tutorial training program ground in learning assistance theory, critical pedagogy and composition theory; managing a 85K budget; and creating partnerships with faculty and academic departments. In addition, the incumbent must possess experience assessing and evaluating academic support programs.

Requirement & Qualifications:

Six years experience teaching and/or tutor training, and managing and administering academic support programs. Possess a thorough knowledge of learning assistance theory, critical pedagogy and composition theory for both developing composition and writing within and across disciplines. Demonstrate cultural competencies working with immigrant students, English second language learners and first generation students. Possess knowledge of learning center theory and experience working in a highly competitive research institution. Have experience working effectively with a racial, linguistically and economically diverse student population.

Other:
This position is designated as sensitive and requires a successful completion of a criminal background check.

Add Job to Basket   Job Basket
Return to Job Postings

"How was your day?" [hopeful]

"Long. How was yours?" [tired]

"Not bad." [lying]

"What'd you do?" [very tired]

"Not much." [true]

"Did you go to the gym?" [half-interested]

"Yeah."

"How was it?"

"The same as always." [bored]

"Did you see anyone?" [trying harder]

"Ran into Charlie."

"How's Charlie?" [interested]

"The same."

"So what else did you do?"

"I dropped off dry cleaning." [pleased]

"Thanks, thanks so much. That helps." [sincere]

"I wanna help."

"I wish you really could." [accidentally on purpose]

"What do you mean?" [hurt]

"Nothing." [lying]

"What did you mean?"

"I only meant that it's hard right now." [soft]

"I know."

"Mostly hard for you."

"That's not true." [tearful]

"But also hard for me."

"I know."

"I took on an extra project." [pained]

"Do you have to?"

"I think we need the money. What do you think?" [bitter]

"I'm looking for a job." [earnest]

"It's hard to find a job." [sympathetic]

"I think I found something." [cautious]

"Really?" [doubtful]

"There's an opening for a grounds custodian." [embarrassed]

"I don't think they'll hire you."

"Why?"

"Because they want immigrants. People who are desperate for work, can't speak English, don't complain. Would you say that describes you?" [laughing]

"Almost, but I speak English."

"Why don't you look in one of the writing departments?"

"I saw one job, but I couldn't decipher the job description."

"We should redo your resume."

"I've been working on it."

"I'm sorry, Frank. But I'm wiped out. I've got an early morning meeting. I'll help you over the weekend."

"Thanks."

"No, it's nothing, honey. It's just that I'm tired now. I can't think about one more thing."

"I know." [resigned]

"I know you know." [resigned]

"We're doing our best."

"Yes."

"I know."

OFF TO PROTEST WITH PETER
SEE YOU LATER!
FRANK TELLER

Lynn called. SAT dinner off. Flu.

PS — You signed FRANK TELLER? I know who you are! Haha!

Dear Laurie,

Let me say it again! The whole family thanks you for everything you've been doing for Frankie! And we trust you!

But I have a couple of concerns. I'm worried because he doesn't tell me much. He says EVERYTHING is fine. The doctors are pleased. The therapists are pleased. The rehab is going well. That's how he talks to me. And I talk back to him the same way. But I can't help feeling in my gut he's protecting me. Protecting me from what?

Yesterday he told me he's going back to work. Is that true? I hope to God it's true. He said Crown Hollow might reopen its doors. He'll get his old job back. Everything I read in the papers tells me those companies are out of business. Period! Kaput! I don't know what Frankie is going to do. Can't rehab help him figure it out?

Enclosed is a little something for the two of you. I wish it was more. Maybe you can treat Frankie to something for me. What's he like to do these days? That's what I don't know. He says he's busy but I can't get much out of him. Maybe he can get a part-time job and write a book. That would give him a real boost. I don't want to impose but over the weekend could you give me call when he's not around? Then maybe we can discuss it personally.

We love you, *Dad*

Thurs
11 pm

YOU PARKED YOUR BUTT
IN MY DRIVEWAY ASS HOLE
NEXT TIME I'LL HAVE IT TOWED

FACILE-T CORP!
EMPLOYMENT APPLICATION

Name
Address
City   State   Zip
Phone
Education   (last year of school completed)
Position preference

English is your 1st language?   ____ Yes   ____ No
Other languages:

Employment Experience

Are you computer literate?   ___ Yes   ___ No

List what computer programs you know:

Have you been fired by any subsidiary of Taniff Corporation in the last three (3) years?

Check one. ___ Yes ___ No

Expected salary (circle one): $12/hr $16/hr $20/hr

Previous Employment History

#1 Company Name (most recent)
Contact
Address
City   State   Zip
TEL   email
Position
How long employed?
Why did you leave?

#2 Company Name
Contact
Address
City   State   Zip
TEL   email
Position
How long employed?
Why did you leave?

[back of employment application]

Customer Service Quiz

A customer calls to complain about the bill. *Please check all that apply.*
__ Have the customer wait while you check the account
__ Make correct alterations to the account
__ Contact your supervisor
__ All of the above

A customer calls about a return. *Please check all that apply.*
__ Tell them there are no returns, only credits
__ Ask customer reason for dissatisfaction
__ Tell customer they can get reduced price for same item
__ Try to interest customer in another product or promotion
__ Contact your supervisor
__ All of the above

Thank you for your interest in joining the FACILE-T CORP! team.
Please apply early and often!

The Human Resources Department will keep your application on file for six (6) months. If during that time, we do not contact you, please feel free to complete another application.

REFERENCES:

SOMETHING WE ALL NEED TO KNOW. IS IT A STROKE?

Sometimes symptoms of a stroke are difficult to identify. Unfortunately, the lack of awareness spells disaster. The stroke victim may suffer brain damage when people nearby fail to recognize the symptoms of a stroke. Now doctors say a bystander can recognize a stroke by asking three simple questions:

– Ask the individual to SMILE.
– Ask him or her to RAISE BOTH ARMS.
– Ask the person to SPEAK A SIMPLE SENTENCE.

If he or she has trouble with any of these tasks, call 9-1-1 immediately and describe the symptoms to the dispatcher.

6:45 am
TGIF
LET'S GO
TO MOVIE
TONIGHT
I love you!

On the back of my note:

                    JACK
                STATE HIST
            2400 London Ran
             Glen Ellen, CA

PARK INFORMATION
Welcome to Jack Lon
State Historic Park
known as Jack Londo
"Beauty Ranch." The
offers 1400+ acres
the Beauty Ranch, m
Wolf House Ruins a
miles of trail. We
that you take 3 hou
but if your time is
suggest 3 different
tours of the part. W
purchasing a park b
to aid in your self-
through the past.

I saw myself half-dressed at gym today. My bra and panties are so ugly, I started to laugh. Remember when we first started? You told me I had to do something about my underwear. You put in an emergency order to VS. I never had boyfriends who cared about underwear. The men I knew only cared what was underneath. I was such a disappointment. So bad at sexy. So silly parading around. I could never take it seriously. It always felt like a joke or prop. But you liked it.

FACILE-T CORP!
EMPLOYMENT APPLICATION

Name   Franklin Teller
Address   506 Carmel Ave
City Albany   State CA   Zip 94706
Phone   (510) 524-3088
Education 19 (last year of school completed) MASTERS POLITICAL SCIENCE
Position preference   WHATEVER IS AVAILABLE

English is your 1st language?   X Yes ___ No
Other languages: French, Russian, studying Arabic

Employment Experience
Are you computer literate?   X Yes ___ No
List what computer programs you know: WORD,EXCEL,PHOTOSHOP
Have you been fired by any subsidiary of Taniff Corporation in
the last three (3) years?
Check one. __ Yes ___ No   DON'T KNOW
Expected salary (circle one): $12/hr $16/hr $20/hr

Previous Employment History
#1 Company Name (most recent)   Crown Hollow Software
Contact   Louise Henderson
Address   130 Third Street
City San Francisco   State CA   Zip 94112
TEL disconnected   email disconnected
Position   Publications Manager
How long employed? 6.5 years
Why did you leave? complicated

#2 Company Name   AAA Software
Contact   Jerry Bruning
Address   Hollis Street
City Emeryville   State CA   Zip ??
TEL (510) 444-4444   email ??
Position   TECH writer
How long employed? 6 months
Why did you leave? personal

[back of employment application]

Customer Service Quiz

A customer calls to complain about the bill. *Please check all that apply.*
   _x_Have the customer wait while you check the account
   _x_Make correct alterations to the account
   _x_Contact your supervisor
   _x_All of the above

A customer calls about a return. *Please check all that apply.*
   __Tell them there are no returns, only credits
   __Ask customer reason for dissatisfaction
   __Tell customer they can get reduced price for same product
   __Try to interest customer in another product or promotion
   __Contact your supervisor
   __All of the above
Is this a trick question?

Thank you for your interest in joining the FACILE-T CORP! team.
Please apply early and often!

The Human Resources Department will keep your application on file for six (6) months. If during that time, we do not contact you, please feel free to complete another application.

REFERENCES:

Laurie Willits, KPK Management, Walnut Creek
(925) 676-5400, ext. ?? (I'm blanking)

FACILE-T CORP! * 2222 Harbour Way South * RICHMOND CALIFORNIA 94802 *
510-215-8666

You look bright in your new shirt and jeans. A big relief for me to see you caring about your appearance. The pot stickers were better than usual. I could eat Chinese food every night. The movie was funny. I haven't heard you belly laugh in a long time. Thank the gods, I almost wept, FRANK TELLER IS LAUGHING! Woody always makes us laugh at his characters' expense. He belittles everyone which annoys me. Especially when I see what you're struggling with. I never belittle you. Even when it's funny. When you can't figure out how to make the toaster work, it makes us both laugh. But not AT you. I just wish I could do better. You deserve nothing but love and support.

Dear Editor:

I am aware there's a gag order on newspapers and reporters. I am aware the American public has been dismissed as well as deceived. Those of us who know better get our news from abroad. That's a pitiful but true state of affairs.

No paper dares challenge the lies from the White House, but I strongly suspect there are no weapons and no threat. Meanwhile, we are supposed to be UNITED. Whatever happened to peaceful division? That used to make me proud of America! PEACEFUL - DIVISION!

In light of the attacks on Muslim Americans or anyone mistaken for Muslim, at least you can try to reduce prejudices instead of fomenting them. Your newspaper constantly refers to Muslims as Arabs or Arab and Muslim. Please do not refer to a terrorist criminal by a religious or ethnic identity. Americans are ignorant enough without you making it worse.

Sincerely,
Franklin Teller
(subscriber for 20 years)
Albany, California

Frank's sign for the protest:

> *WAR   IS*
>
> *THE   HEALTH*
>
> *OF   THE   STATE!*
>
> *— Randolph Bourne*

"Are you OK?" [concerned]

"I'm tired, that's all."

"Big week."

"And next week, too." [depressed]

"What do you wanna do this weekend?" [timid]

[long silence]

"Did you hear me?"

"I heard you."

"Wanna go to Pt. Reyes?"

"I don't wanna drive so far."

"How about a hike with Jane and Eddie in Tilden? That's not far."

"I don't really wanna see anyone."

"Because you're tired?"

"I need to rest up for my meetings."

"Can I help?"

"Not with the meetings."

"No, I didn't mean that." [discouraged]

"Can't you go hiking without me?"

"I just thought you might wanna see the new baby."

"I'd love to . . . but just staying home, quiet."

"What about my resume?"

"I can look it over tomorrow. What about the job application?"

"I have it."

"Do you want me to review it?"

"So you don't wanna go to the Adlers?"

"They called?" [surprised]

"I told you, didn't I?" [unsure]

"I don't think so."

"They're having a BBQ on Sunday."

"What did you say?"

"I said I'd ask you."

"Do you wanna go?"

"Not without you?" [bashful]

"But do you wanna go?"

"I was thinking Bill might know of a job."

"That's a good idea."

"Maybe he's hiring drivers."

"Is driving safe?" [concerned]

"The doctor said it's fine. [angry] What's your problem?"

"Don't you have to get clearance?"

"I meet with DMV next week. Then I can drive all I fucking want."

"Frank!"

"Well, what should I tell Bill?"

"Tell him we can come. Ask what we should bring."

Part 2

YOU ARE INVITED
TO A REUNION
OF THE BUCKS
OF YESTERYEAR

Sunday, May 17

Shutters on the Beach
One Pico
Santa Monica
6 pm - Cocktails
7 pm - Dinner

BE THERE OR
ZIGGARAUT!

RSVP by April 21
Harold Betz
cell 310-567-8889
harold190SL@aol.com
$75 per person

Thurs
11 pm

YOU PARKED YOUR BUTT
IN MY DRIVEWAY ASS HOLE
NEXT TIME I'LL HAVE IT TOWED

Is this from our new neighbor?

LJW

Dear Simon —

I know we've moved on.
Long ago. But we always said
we could count on each other's love,
I still take you at your word.

It's too much to explain
in a note. Frank has been sick.
Maybe you heard. Of course it is
hardest on him. But hard on me too.
In one minute our life turned
on its head. You know how I am.
I can handle it but it's totally
overwhelming.

Anyway I thought
we might get together.
Not that I want to burden you.
This is my load.
But I'd love to see you.
We always had such fun.
Even our toughest moments
were fun. If you have the time
and inclination, call me at work,
925-676-5400 ext. 103.

Love, Laurie

FRANK!

bombs won't STOP
because YOU refuse to sleep
turn off TV & get to bed
PLEASE

Actions/Events of the South Bay Mobilization -
Educate, Involve & Mobilize for Peace & Justice

Demands to Prosecute U.S. Criminals
for Genocide, War Crimes,
Crimes Against Peace and Humanity

Presented to the U.S. Attorney
U.S. Department of Justice
at the Federal Building
San Jose, California

By
Representatives of
The South Bay Mobilization to Stop the War
480 North First Street, Suite 205
San Jose, CA 95103
408-998-8504

Demands to Prosecute U.S. Criminals for Genocide, War Crimes, Crimes Against Peace and Humanity

On behalf of the member countries of the United Nations and the people of the United States and the World, demand is hereby made on the United States Department of Justice to exercise its authority to investigate and prosecute all those responsible for the crimes of genocide, crimes against humanity and war crimes committed by those who planned, supported and carried out the initial Gulf War, the 12 years of sanctions and the currently pre-emptive war with Iraq. The crimes outlined below are in violation of the Genocide Convention Implementation Act of 1987, the Geneva Conventions, the Principles of the Nuremberg Trials and the United Nations Charter. As such, they are violations of both the laws of the United States and of the international community. In addition, we demand that an injunction against all aspects of this pre-emptive war be immediately implemented until said investigation and prosecution is completed. . . .

I.   Specific Charges Under U.S. Law: the Genocide Convention Implementation Act of 1987

A.   Charges Under 18 USC 1091 (a) (1). . . .

Under this provision, we charge the following violations:

1.   Bombing the civilian infrastructure, specifically the electrical grid, water system and water treatment facilities in Iraq with full knowledge of the widespread water-born diseases that would result in a decimation of the civilian population, specifically the children of Iraq, resulted in conditions of life that were intended to physically destroy the Iraqi people. . . .

B.   Charges Under 18 USC 1091 (a) (3). . . .

Under this provision, we charge the following violations:

1.   The massive bombardment of Iraq, under "Operation Shock & Awe," is planned to drop over 6,000 bombs on Iraq over the first two days of the war, with the specific intent of producing widespread terror through the Iraqi population. . . .

2.   The devastating effects of the widespread death of children. . . .

C.   Charges Under 18 USC 1091 (a) (2). . . .

Under this provision, we charge the following violations:

1.   The specific targeting of the civilian infrastructure. . . .

2.   The continued use of sanctions for the past 12 years. . . .

II. Specific Charges for Violations of International Law under the United Nations Charter, the Geneva Convention and Nuremberg Conventions

A.   Charges Under the United Nations Charter. . . .

B.   Charges Under the Geneva Conventions. . . .

C.   Charges Under the Principles of the Nuremberg Tribunals. . . .

Murder, extermination, enslavement, deportation and other inhuman acts done against any civilian population, or persecutions on political, racial or religious grounds. . . .

In light of the forgoing charges, we demand an immediate injunction against the further planning and carrying out of this invasion and an immediate enforcement of the United Nations Charter, Geneva Conventions and the Principles of the Nuremberg Tribunals against the following individuals:

1. President George W. Bush
2. Vice President Richard Cheney
3. Secretary of Defense Donald Rumsfeld
4. Secretary of State Colin Powell
5. Every member of Congress that voted to give President Bush their War Powers responsibilities
6. General Tommy Franks, Commander of the United States forces in the Persian Gulf
7. Former Secretary of State Madeleine Albright
8. Former President of the United States George Herbert Walker Bush
9. Former President William Clinton
10. General Norman Schwartzkof. . . .

With Sincerity,
The South Bay Mobilization to Stop the War

TO: FRANKLIN TELLER
sonofabitchexcellente

YOU better be at MOTHERSUCKER Reunite
cause I am treating Gangof8 to 18 holes

Guess you heard Bruce died
I was sorry you missed memorial
It didn't feel right without you there

Saw your dad the other day
I was in my new ride
He said it was the car
your mother always wanted
I remember your mother
Wasn't she hot?
JUST KIDDING!

Hey, call me on my cell and tell me your flight
I'll come get you, I swear
I love you, man
Don't let me down the way you used to
JUST KIDDING!

Harold / 323-777-BETZ

You wish . . . you wish you could go back and be well again . . . you wish we loved each other like the first minute we met . . . you wish we had kids . . . you wish you could find a job . . . you wish . . . you wish. . . .

FRANKIE, Found on web thought you'd be interested!
GO GET 'EM! Love, *Dad*

"How to Write a Best-Seller?"
by Suzy Lipton

OK. Hands up. Who wants to write a best-seller? Nearly everyone!
Let's discuss the ingredients for a best-seller.

√ The stakes MUST be high! You need to base your plot around a story of life vs. death; happiness vs. tragedy; fulfillment of a life's dream vs. so on.

√ Your characters must be larger than life. Here are some suggestions. A hero can be tall and powerfully built, not necessarily handsome, but definitely "craggy." Your heroine can be either drop-dead gorgeous, or very cute. Remember a nice pair of tits never go out of fashion. Don't forget that one must be extremely wealthy and the other impoverished in proportion to the privilege of the other. Let your hero and heroine clash at the beginning, and then after many ups and downs realize their destinies are entwined.

√ Your settings should be exotic and filled with lots of detail. Colors, plants, animals, clothes. Remember you don't need to transport your readers to the Walmart. They prefer to visit the Caribbean or Amazonian rainforest or Arctic circle, or even outer space! Nobody says fiction has to be realistic!

If you set your hero in present time, it's more likely to be optioned for film. Remember costume dramas are expensive.

√ Search for topical themes on the Internet. Maybe climate change or white-collar crime.

√ Be sure to include car chases, powerful confrontations, and coincidence. Remember me when you get your six-figure advance!

———————————————

Suzy Lipton is a professional best-selling authoress who offers her clients all editorial services.

Questions:

1. How many worldwide marched to stop the war?
2. How many wanted to march and didn't?
3. How many people live where they can't march?

Answers:

1. eloep noillim ytriht tsael ta
2. ynam taht semit net ebyam
3. sseltnuoc

CAN YOU READ MY CODE?

30 million? AMAZING!
But why are you writing in code?

FACILE-T CORP!
EMPLOYMENT APPLICATION

Name   Franklin Teller
Address   506 Carmel Ave
City   Albany   State   CA   Zip   94706
Phone   (510) 524-3088
Education ~~19~~ (last year of school completed)   **TOO HIGH**
Position preference   ~~WHATEVER IS AVAILABLE~~   **BE SPECIFIC**
English is your 1st language? X Yes ___ No   **OVEREDUCATED**
Other languages: ~~French, Russian, studying Arabic~~

Employment Experience
Are you computer literate? X Yes ___ No
List what computer programs you know: WORD, EXCEL, PHOTOSHOP
Have you been fired by any subsidiary of Taniff Corporation in the last three (3) years?
Check one. ___ Yes ___ No ~~DON'T KNOW~~   **check NO**
Expected salary (circle one): $12/hr $16/hr $20/hr   **ASK for more**

Previous Employment History
#1 Company Name (most recent)   Crown Hollow Software
Contact   Louise Henderson
Address   130 Third Street
City   San Francisco   State   CA   Zip   94112
TEL   disconnected   email lbh@earthlink.net
Position   Publications Manager
How long employed? 6.5 years
Why did you leave? ~~complicated story~~   **NO LONGER IN BUSINESS**

#2 Company Name   AAA Software
Contact Jerry Bruning
Address   Hollis Street
City   Emeryville   State   CA   Zip ?? **LOOK UP**
TEL   (510) 444-4444   email ~~??~~
Position   TECH writer
How long employed?   6 months
Why did you leave? ~~personal~~   **BETTER JOB OPPORTUNITY**

[back of employment application]

Customer Service Quiz

A customer calls to complain about the bill. *Please check all that apply.*
    _x_Have the customer wait while you check the account
    __Make correct alterations to the account
    _x_Contact your supervisor
    __All of the above

A customer calls about a return. *Please check all that apply.*
    __Tell them there are no returns, only credits
    _x_Ask customer reason for dissatisfaction
    __Tell customer they can get reduced price for same product
    _x_Try to interest customer in another product or promotion
    __Contact your supervisor
    __All of the above
    ~~Is this a trick question?~~

Thank you for your interest in joining the FACILE-T CORP! team.
Please apply early and often!

The Human Resources Department will keep your application on file for six (6) months. If during that time, we do not contact you, please feel free to complete another application.

REFERENCES:

Laurie Willits, KPK Management, Walnut Creek, <u>ADD</u> CA 94598
(925) 676-5400, ext. ~~?? (I'm blanking)~~ 103

"How did you sleep?"

"Well, not so bad." [laughing]

"Are you feeling better?"

"I'm rested. But worried about you."

"Worried?" [disingenuous]

"I wish you weren't so unhappy."

"Happiness isn't everything."

"No." [thoughtful]

"When I worked at the mental hospital, a patient told me it wasn't that much better being happy. She'd tried it."

"You've told me that story." [laughing]

"When I was a boy, I thought we had to choose."

"Choose happiness?"

"No, choose between happiness and freedom."

"Doesn't freedom make you happy?"

"Not necessarily." [pause]

"You were happy when we met." [coy]

"I was ecstatic."

"So was I." [quiet]

"I think you're right."

"About what?"

"About happiness. It is important."

"But it's only a moment."

"And life is?"

"Life is what happens between moments."

Dear Dr. Mayer:

I thought it best that I write and then perhaps you can contact Frank directly. I don't want him to think I've put you up to it. However, I am alarmed. He has started writing backwards. Is that typical of neurological trauma? I'll enclose a sample of something. I think it's a challenge (mental exercise) to write backwards so I'm not as concerned about the activity as the reason he gives when I ask. He says it's code. He says he has to write in code. He is very upset about the political situation, but I'm afraid he's losing perspective. Is that part of neurological trauma? He also remains depressed. Sadness at least seems alive, but Frank is so listless. Unanimated. Could it be a side effect of the medication? I think he needs to see you, but I don't feel right calling the nurse and saying it's an emergency. He has been like this for a couple of months so it's not exactly an emergency. The code thing is new.

Can you please call me at work so we can discuss it in private? Thank you.

Sincerely,
Laurie Willits
925-676-5400 ext. 103

PS. Dr. Mayer, This is a sample of what I'm talking about. It's Frank's note to his friend:

dratsabuoyzteb
maisabmudsaerauoysihtdaernacuoyfi
noinuerehtotgnimocmaiesruocfo

Thank you again.

LJW

Dear Helen and Bill —
There's nothing else that measures up
to a party at your house.

I know you haven't seen Frank since
the stroke, and while he has made
great strides, sometimes his words
don't come out the way he wants.

Helen, Frank wanted to write this
himself to apologize for his remarks
about your blouse, but he was worried
he'd say the wrong thing. That's part
of the problem. He's struggling and
because he looks normal, everyone
forgets there is a problem. He can't
always say what he means – and
most important, what he says
doesn't accurately reflect what he thinks.
He didn't mean anything at all, and
I hope you'll understand that it's
one of the sad parts of the condition.
It still could get better. We're hoping.

Thanks so much for including us at your party.

Love, Laurie

ALTA BATES

MEDICAL CENTER

OUTPATIENT REHABILITATION
NEUROPSYCHOLOGICAL CONSULTATION REPORT

<u>NAME</u>:	Franklin Teller
<u>AGE</u>:	48 years
<u>HANDEDNESS:</u>	Right
<u>EDUCATION</u>:	Masters-Poli Sci
<u>OCCUPATION</u>:	Software Publisher
<u>EXAMINER:</u>	Elaine Martin, Ph.D.
<u>REFERRED BY</u>:	Benjamin Mayer, M.D.

PROCEDURES:
Clinical Interview
Animal Naming Test
Boston Naming Test
California Verbal Learning Test (CVLT)
Controlled Oral Word Association Test
Paced Auditory Serial Addition Test (PASAT)
Proverbs Test
Rey Osterrieth Complex Figure
Stroop Color Word Test
Trailmaking Test A and B
Wechsler Adult Intelligence Scale -- III (WAIS-III)
Wechsler Memory Scale -- Revised, Abbreviated (WMS-R)
Wisconsin Card Sort Test (WCST)

IDENTIFICATION: The patient is a 48-year old, right-handed, Caucasian gentleman who was on a business trip to Washington, DC, when he sustained an episode in which he was unable to walk and noted a change in his speech. He was admitted to George Washington University Hospital (900 23rd Street Northwest, Washington, DC 20037) where he was evidencing partial paralysis of the right side of his body. An MRI of the brain administered during the course of this hospitalization indicated multiple old right hemisphere lesions in the basal ganglion as well as a current new lesion in the left basal ganglion. Mr. Teller remained in the hospital for a period of eight days and reportedly improved in terms of the paralysis and speech. He was placed on Coumadin prophylactically and returned to the Bay Area.

When initially seen by this examiner in October, the patient continued to complain of changes in his mentation which were exceedingly anxiety provoking to him. The reported changes included decreased attention and concentration noted when reading, decreased comprehension, commission of a number of errors in reading, and difficulty writing due to poor thought formulation as well as mechanics. Mr. Teller also reported extreme fatigability, subjective feelings of depression and a noted change in his dream pattern in that he no longer dreamt during sleep.

BEHAVIORAL OBSERVATIONS: Mr. Teller was a casually groomed, well-nourished, Caucasian gentleman who appeared his chronological age. He was initially seen by this examiner in early and middle November at the request of the speech pathologist who was treating him due to her concerns about both his cognitive as well as emotional functioning. On the first occasion, November 3, Mr. Teller appeared exceedingly depressed and anxious.

TEST RESULTS: Mr. Teller's results are presented according to different components of cognition (e.g., attention, language, memory, etc.). An emphasis is placed on describing test results.

ATTENTION/CONCENTRATION: Mr. Teller's auditory attention for simple information falls into the high average to very superior range. On Digits Forwards, he achieved a score in the 99th percentile while on Digits Backwards, his score fell into the 90th percentile.

SPEECH AND LANGUAGE: The patient completed the Proverbs Test in which he was required to interpret a series of 12 proverbs. On this test, his writing was exceedingly micrographic but relatively well organized in terms of thought formulation. His interpretations of proverbs were at times concrete. For example, "one swallow does not make a summer" was interpreted by him to mean, "a season is composed of many things."

MEMORY: Fund of general information, assessed by the Information subtest of the WAIS-III was found to be in the high average to superior range and commensurate with likely premorbid abilities.

FRONTAL LOBE OR EXECUTIVE FUNCTIONS: Organizational problems are noted both in his expressive language as well as when he is presented with a complex figure, the Rey Osterrieth, and required to organize his copy strategy in order to render an accurate and reasonable reproduction.

SUMMARY IMPRESSIONS: On formal neuropsychological testing, Mr. Teller's performance is consistent with what appears to be a frontal subcortical cerebral dysfunction which, although bilateral, has significant right hemisphere features.

Mr. Teller is being followed by Dr. Mayer to further investigate the etiology of these strokes in a rather young and well-functioning gentleman.

"I know you don't want to hear this."

"Then why say it?"

"Because I care about you."

"If you cared about me. . . ."

"Because I think it's important."

"To you everything is important."

"What's that mean?"

"You put your fucking nose in everybody's business."

"Frank!"

"I'm sorry."

"Accepted."

"What? Am I eating too much grease?"

"I gave up on your diet."

"My cholesterol is perfect."

"I don't care about potato chips."

"Anyway I cut down."

"Thank you."

"You're welcome. Was that what you wanted?"

"No, it has to do with this backwards thing."

"It's good mental exercise."

"I wish you felt better."

"I feel OK. I went to the gym today."

"I mean better about yourself . . . as a person."

"As a person? Instead of a squirrel?"

"I'm trying to be serious."

"Me, too. Sometimes I feel like a squirrel."

"You hate squirrels."

"That doesn't mean I can't feel like one."

"That's my point. You choose an animal you hate."

"I don't hate them. I just wish the fuck they'd get out of my yard."

"I don't want to talk about squirrels."

"Me either. Ever."

"I wish you liked yourself more."

"Myself? I'm not myself so how can I like me?"

"Frank, but you're still so many wonderful things."

"Yeah? I can't seem to figure those out."

"You have to believe you're going to get better."

"See, you have faith."

"Not in God."

"Faith in something."

"Faith in man."

"That's a mistake."

"Faith in . . . I don't know."

"You think things work out."

"I think things change. You're changing. You're getting better."

"How do you know?"

"I feel it. I see it."

"How?"

"You can do so much more than you could even a few months ago."

"Like?"

"That's the problem. You can't remember how you were. But I remember. When I first came to the hospital, you couldn't move your right side. You couldn't count backwards by 7. You didn't know the capital of Ohio."

"OK, Columbus. I'm a genius."

"Anyway I wanted to talk about . . . going away."

"A trip?"

"I think it would be good."

"Can we afford a trip?"

"I think it would be good for me."

"To take a trip?"

"I think it would be good for me to go off."

"Without me?"

"For a weekend."

"But we haven't been away."

"Two nights."

"To get away from me."

"No, Frank. To be quiet with myself for a bit."

"This is harder on you than me."

"No, that's not it. I need to get away from work, the house."

"And me."

"Don't take it personally."

"How am I supposed to take it?"

"Understand I have to clear my head sometimes."

"I'm sorry."

"I don't want to complain."

"You should. You should talk to somebody."

"No, you should talk to somebody. You should be in therapy."

"I don't have anything to say."

"You have plenty to say."

"I can't find the words anymore to say it."

"That's your excuse."

"It's not an excuse."

"Anytime I need to talk to you, you say you can't follow along."

"That's true."

"Dr. Mayer recommended a therapist."

"You spoke to him?"

"Briefly."

"Why didn't he call me?"

"I contacted him. I thought he could help."

"You said I was crazy?"

"No."

"You said I was driving you crazy?"

"No."

"You said I needed a therapist?"

"I asked if there was someone he knew."

"He knows thousands."

"Someone he trusted."

"And?"

"I have a couple of names."

"They're going to put me on Prozac."

"Maybe it could help."

"That's all they do now. I'd rather take LSD."

"Promise me, you won't do something foolish like that."

"I'll make you a deal. LSD or Emmanthaler?"

"Frank, be serious."

"I am serious."

You've been to cities built by the water where instead of highways there are boulevards lined with palms. The railroad tracks are far from the river or sea so nothing ugly interrupts the beauty. Cities like Capetown and Rio. You've been to Baghdad and Kabul. That's why you travel—to make places and people real. Now when you hear the Tigris is in flames, your memories burn, too.

LJW

Dear Simon —

It was a treat to see you.
I hope I didn't complain too much.
These days it only takes one beer
to get me going. Better not try that at work.

But you, as usual, were very understanding.
I'm not quite sure I can handle this,
but it really doesn't matter.
I have to handle it.

Except for your son's operation,
things are great.
"Top of your game"
isn't that the expression?
I'm happy for your success
with the band. European tour sounds
grand & I was flattered you asked
me to come along. Groupie? Roadie?

I laugh to myself whenever
I picture the time I met you
at the airport wearing only
my raincoat & high heels.
OK, I'm getting sentimental
which is never a good thing.

I'll close with thanks
again for lunch.
Next time, my treat.

Love, Laurie

PS -- Best to call my work #

Today is like the others. There's a perpetual garden of flowers in bloom and finches pecking at the thistle sacks outside the window. I like the rain. The air is clean. I smell the sea. I smell the ground. The smells rush through me as if I'd just been born. When I was little, I use to snuggle in the dirt like a pig. I haven't changed. I love to walk and garden and swim in the rain. It's raining. I'm so happy I don't have to go to work. My only misery is seeing you. If only I could drag you away from the TV. You sit in that dark room, day and night, crying over the war. You go to the computer so you can see children in hospitals, blown up and burned. You cry over the ruins. I can't bear it when you cry. I have no way to comfort you. What can I say to you? What can I do for you? Inside I'm crying, too. We should all be crying. The whole world should be crying. But you can't cry for everyone, Frank. You have to come outside into the garden. Smell the flowers. Smell the air. You have to feel there's hope. Don't you? Don't you have to feel there's some way to forget the nightmare for a minute?

War Is the Health of the State
by Randolph Bourne

Excerpts from the first part of an essay entitled "The State," left unfinished at Bourne's untimely death in 1918.

. . . . The Government, with no mandate from the people, without consultation of the people, conducts all the negotiations, the backing and filling, the menaces and explanations, which slowly bring it into collision with some other Government, and gently and irresistibly slides the country into war. . . .

The moment war is declared, however, the mass of the people, through some spiritual alchemy, become convinced that they have willed and executed the deed themselves. They then, with the exception of a few malcontents, proceed to allow themselves to be regimented, coerced, deranged in all the environments of their lives, and turned into a solid manufactory of destruction toward whatever other people may have, in the appointed scheme of things, come within the range of the Government's disapprobation. . . .

Country is a concept of peace, of tolerance, of living and letting live. But State is essentially a concept of power, of competition: it signifies a group in its aggressive aspects. And we have the misfortune of being born not only into a country but into a State, and as we grow up we learn to mingle the two feelings into a hopeless confusion. . . .

War is the health of the State. It automatically sets in motion throughout society those irresistible forces for uniformity, for passionate cooperation with the Government in coercing into obedience the minority groups and individuals which lack the larger herd sense. . . .

http://struggle.ws/hist_texts/warhealthstate1918.html

Frank my man

Still have not heard SQUAT
at least not in English
are you NUTS?

And will you PLEASE let me know
IF WHEN HOW you're coming
I can't wait to introduce
you to my new girl
she's a hottie

If you and Laurie need
place to stay I got it

Now call me damn it
we tee off 8 am

Harold / 323-777-BETZ

LJW

Frank darling —

*For your birthday present I found a copy of <u>Inanna, Queen
of Heaven and Earth: Her Stories and Hymns from Sumer</u>.
Recommended by Alice Hutchinson, she teaches Middle
Eastern Studies at UC.*

*I think it's the oldest poetry we have, 2000 BC! Inanna's
journey to the underworld and love poems from her to
Dumuzi. If you look at the map where Inanna thrived, modern
Baghdad is just north of Babylon.*

*Maybe we can read it aloud to each other on the drive
down. So many wonderful things in store for you during the
next year.*

Happy Birthday!
All my love, Laurie

LJW

Harold, Don't despair.
Your oldest friend is
on his way. If he hasn't
written, don't fret.

We're driving. We're
staying with our friend Kim.

We'll see you soon. Don't count
on Frank for golf. He can't grip
with his right hand.

Love, Laurie

You met Kim when you met me at the Nordstrom's accessories counter, trying to pick out a Mother's Day gift. You chose a pair of black lace gloves that buttoned at the wrist, and although we tried to tell you women no longer wear impractical gloves, you insisted. It was sexy to meet a man buying a beautiful, useless gift for his mother. You didn't say you were married, but when you came back the next month, you said you were divorced. You said the gloves were inspired by a Joan Crawford film. After I met your mother, I realized it was a way to distance her inside the pantheon of movie stars from that era when some women were truly terrifying.

You asked Kim out first. I don't blame you. I adore Kim. I'm happy we'll see her soon.

Marilyn is moving in with her boyfriend and here are the discards. Please ask Jess if she wants anything?

IKEA furniture (see website)	Unit Price	Total
6 Roger chairs	59.00	354.00
4 Nikolaus folding chairs	29.99	111.96
2 Stig bar stools	24.99	49.98
2 Jussi tables	129.00	258.00
1 Mysinge couch	299.00	299.00
2 Klappsta living room chairs	118.00	236.00
1 Anlang table lamp	19.99	19.99

Inanna spoke:

"What I tell you,
Let the singer weave into song.
What I tell you,
Let it flow from ear to mouth,
Let it pass from old to young:
My vulva, the horn,
The boat of Heaven,
Is full of eagerness like the young moon.
My untilled land lies fallow.

As for me, Inanna,
Who will plow my vulva?
Who will plow my high field?
Who will plow my wet ground?

As for me the young woman,
Who will plow my vulva?
Who will station the ox there?
Who will plow my vulva?"

Dumuzi replied:

"Great Lady, the king will plow your vulva.
I, Dumuzi the King, will plow your vulva."

Inanna:

"Then plow my vulva, man of my heart!
Plow my vulva!"

At the king's lap stood the rising cedar.
Plants grew high by their side.
Grains grew high by their side.
Gardens flourished luxuriantly.

Inanna sang:

"He has sprouted; he has burgeoned;
He is lettuce planted by the water.
He is the one my womb loves best."

It depressed us both, the ploughing, the vulva, the burgeoning, the lettuce. We laughed, but it depressed us. Except for the historical commentary, you said you didn't want me to read. It was a sad reminder of our own buried passions. Once we regarded each other as the two most desirable creatures in the world. I think it's my fault. You think it's yours. You take it as a sign I don't love you, but that's not true. I love you intensely, but I can't possibly love you the way I did. You think you're undesirable. You blame yourself. I blame our familiarity. It's easy to desire a stranger, but in fact, I don't desire anyone. I'm tired. I don't have the energy for desire. You're tired, too. The illness makes you exhausted, withdrawn, ashamed. As for sex, I'd have to do the work. I don't want to. I don't want to. I don't want to.

"Let me drive."

"I'm good."

"I knew you'd say that."

"What's the problem?"

"You're weaving."

"It doesn't matter."

"It matters."

"There's no traffic."

"The trucks are speeding."

"I'm in the right lane."

"They can't even see us."

"Of course, they see us."

"Pull off at the next exit."

"Why don't you read?"

"It gives me a headache."

"Didn't you bring a tape?"

"Let me drive."

"We're almost there."

"We have two hours."

"I like to drive over the Grapevine."

"I do, too."

"When I was young, it felt like the whole world stretched out in front of me. The Grapevine took my breath away."

"So poetic."

"Naive, you mean. Children and the poets."

"Frank, don't trash it."

"When we're young, most of us don't know what's coming."

"I knew."

"You were wise."

"I saw bad things I wouldn't wish on anyone."

"If we had had a child. . . ."

"I wouldn't wish on anyone."

"This illness makes me feel young. But not in a good way."

"It makes me feel old."

"You can drive."

"Ur-Nammu founded a dynasty at the city of Ur, the so-called Third Dynasty of Ur (approximately 2050-1950 B.C.), that gave promise of an impressive renaissance. . . . He promulgated the first law code in recorded history, a document whose preamble boasts that he, Ur-Nammu, removed the 'chiselers' and grafters from the land, established and regulated honest weights and measures, and saw to it 'that the orphan did not fall a prey to the wealthy, that the widow did not fall a prey to the powerful, that the man of one shekel did not fall a prey to the man of one mina [sixty shekels].'"

At Kim's apartment in Santa Monica.

"I am so glad to see you two."

"Watch out! You'll make Laurie jealous."

"I don't get jealous."

"Really? Remember when?"

"Never mind."

"Dredging up the inglorious past?"

"It wasn't so inglorious."

"The place looks great."

"It does, doesn't it? I changed the mood."

"What inspired you?"

"Because I can't afford to move EVER."

"It's so much warmer."

"That's what I thought. Dump IKEA."

"That's what my friend Marilyn just did."

"Hey, I'll be back in a minute."

"Frank, we just got here."

"It'll only take. . . ."

"Where?"

"I need to run to the drug store."

"Three blocks over."

"I know."

"But I've probably got it."

"Kim, you wouldn't have this."

"What is it, Frank?"

"A surprise."

"You're nuts!"

"She's got that right. When I leave, she'll tell you all about it."

"That's not so."

"Haven't you been comparing crazy boyfriends for twenty years?"

"Frank isn't crazy."

"Of course, he's not."

"Of course, he is. See you in a minute."

"Be careful."

"Go to the light and take a left."

"Frank looks fine."

"Looks are deceiving."

"You look fine."

"I'm toasted."

"You're so pretty. It's hard to hide that."

"Kim, please."

"I'm sure it's difficult."

"Frank has become. . . ."

"What violent?"

"He's so upset about the war."

"Most of the time I live with a bag over my head."

"Maybe we can get him a bag."

"I don't mean to joke."

"He can't think about anything else. I had to twist his arm to come to this reunion."

"High school?"

"The Bucks, it's a social club. Anything to distract him."

"From what?"

"He's obsessed."

"Like how?"

"Like he believes the government is watching him."

"You mean he's paranoid?"

"He thinks about leaving the country."

"Where?"

"Exactly."

"Maybe he just feels bad."

"He feels bad about almost everything, but he feels the worst about the government."

"Sometimes things change."

"Tell me about it."

"I mean maybe they'll be an uprising."

"The whole country is on drugs."

"You can't blame him for being awake."

"I don't blame him. I just worry. I worry he's going off the deep end."

"What do the doctors say?"

"Fine, fine, fine."

"Do you believe them?"

"Would you?"

"Was I gone long enough?"

"Too long."

"You missed me?"

"Yes, we missed you."

"What you'd get?"

"I told you. A surprise."

"We're too curious to wait."

"Did Laurie tell you everything?"

"There wasn't time for everything."

"Did she tell you she met her old boyfriend?"

"Frank, what are you talking about?"

"She didn't mention a thing."

"They were recently seen at the Townhouse."

"Frank!"

"You were, weren't you?"

"What?"

"With Simon?"

"Are you spying on me?"

"It was pure coincidence if you believe in such things."

"I believe in coincidence, Frank."

"You would, Kim. But you believe in astrology, too. And other weirdo stuff."

"Don't put me down for my beliefs, Frank."

"I can't help it."

"Tolerance."

"If only they were tolerant."

"Do you have someone following me around?"

"Frank wouldn't do that."

"Never. I'm too busy being followed. Did she tell you our phone is tapped?"

"Frank, it isn't. I called the telephone company about the noise."

"Laurie believes the phone company."

"Laurie is here in the room."

"Who can you believe?"

"They all lie."

"You can't even believe your mother."

"Especially my mother."

"On the drive I was thinking about those gloves you bought her."

"You did go out with Simon, didn't you?"

"Simon and I are old friends."

"Of course, you are."

"We are."

"So why didn't you tell me?"

"I didn't know you cared."

"You were hiding it."

"Who told you?"

"Jess saw you."

"I didn't see her."

"Maybe you were too engrossed."

"Please, Frank. Simon is. . . ."

"I thought he got divorced."

"Simon only thinks about one thing."

"And it's not Laurie. I can tell you because I once met the guy."

"Why didn't you mention it?"

"It was lunch, Frank. It was nothing."

"I only think about one thing, too."

"That's different."

"Maybe Simon and I should get together."

"He only thinks about himself."

"He's successful and I am?"

"Frank, please. I'm not discussing it."

"You want to be with him?"

"Laurie has stuck by you thick and. . . ."

"Is that what you think, Kim? *Stuck* by me?"

"I'm with you because I want to be."

"That's clear to everyone."

"What's clear is she could have done better."

"Laurie had lots of choices."

"And she chose me?"

"She chose you, Frank."

"I chose you."

You were in the bathroom a long time. The water running in the sink. Then stopping. Then cursing. Then water again.

"You okay, dear?"
"I'm just finishing up."

What in the world does that mean?

Dying your hair was quite the surprise. You said you needed a distinguishing mark.

"But why?" I asked for the second time.

"To separate myself from them," you said.

I remarked the separation was obvious since twenty-five years had passed. I also said the jet black looked awful, but you replied that wasn't the point. Kim, ever eccentric, took your side. She said it was an "affirmation of change," which in her opinion is always a good thing.

I tried to use one of those emotional exercises where you distance yourself from the reality of another person. In this case, you. I told myself I wasn't responsible for your hair. It was your decision. But the exercise didn't really work. I felt it was my fault.

Kim called it "cute." That was totally indulgent. It wasn't at all cute. Maybe it was audacious. Or freaky. Or unexpected. But it wasn't cute.

You said you didn't have anything in common with these friends anymore. But in case they didn't realize it, the hair would make it clear.

Clothing was another unpleasant topic. Kim took your side again. (I wish you'd married Kim). She said you were a grown man and could wear anything you fucking pleased.

I disagreed because it was a nice restaurant. I thought Harold would feel personally insulted. Of all your old friends, Harold has expressed the most concern about you. He offered to loan you money, which by the way, might be necessary someday.

You said you weren't about to kiss up to Betzy by succumbing to a tie. But I hadn't suggested a tie. I just thought shorts and Tevas were too casual.

When Kim said you were a grown man for the third time, I almost shoved my pantyhose in her mouth. That's the other thing. I dressed up which made you look more ridiculous. Or maybe I was the one who looked ridiculous.

"OK," I said, giving up and trying another exercise. "These are your friends. This is your reunion. I don't have to be involved."

"Good for you," Kim said victoriously.

"You look pretty," Frank said to me. All I could do was smirk.

We left a little before six and arrived exactly on time to an empty bar. You ordered a Grey Goose martini. I had a Coke with lime. I figured I better not drink. If anything got out of control, at least I'd have the sense to tell you we had to leave.

We looked out the big picture windows at the ocean. Choppy and gray. A sailboat passed on the horizon. A streak of orange light slipped through the gray blinds of sky.

"I love this time of day," I said.

"Too bad it's overcast."

"You're so negative."

"Was that negative?"

I thought all you have to do is open your pompous mouth for your friends to know you've distanced yourself. Anyway you already betrayed their loyalty by refusing to go to UCLA. To a man, they're Bruins.

Harold and a young woman arrived. Very young. Any embarrassment I had about Frank's hair vanished. Between Crystal's silicon boobs (rising over the neckline of her blouse) and her dimpled ass (hanging out of her Diesel jeans), I didn't think we'd be noticed. After one drink Crystal kicked off her three-inch heels. She was a blabbermouth and no matter what was happening around her, she blabbed on.

"This old fart, Frank Teller, was my best friend since fourth grade," Harold announced. "Can you believe that?"

Crystal looked Frank up and down. She paused a millisecond on the dyed hair and moved to the shorts and Tevas.

"I can't see your toenails because of all the hair. Harold, look at Frank's toes. Can you see his toenails?"

Harold got down on floor. "Yeah, I see them."

"Motherfucker!" you said and ordered another martini.

I tried one of the breathing exercises again. This time it was helpful. While we waited for the other Bucks, Crystal told you her secret formula for getting rid of unwanted hair.

She said you could find it on the web: a paste of frankincense from *The Art of Perfumery* by G.W. Septimus Piesse, published in 1857.

Your friend Harold isn't a bad man. He tries to be considerate. Mostly, he wants to talk about himself. He's had erratic successes in finance. When it goes well, he acts superior. When he's broke, he gets extremely depressed. However, he is never comfortable being himself. That's his biggest problem which leads him to try to be another person. These days he's riding high with a sports car and a sexy young girlfriend.

"Be yourself, Harold! Even if you're an asshole!" He makes me want to shout.

He looks up to you. They all do. They consider you the "intellectual." They expect an honest response if they ask you a question. Sometimes they don't dare ask. That's how fearsome your honesty can be.

Harold wanted everyone to make a little speech as a tribute to old friendships. Harold and Richard Weinberg both spoke about your leadership in the group.

"Not Frank's looks," they teased.

"Or agility and speed," acknowledging your high school record in hurdles.

"Or brains" because they're all fairly smart with the kind of educated smartness that takes its cues from *The New Yorker.*

"But his integrity," Harold stuttered.

"Frank is a stand-up guy." That's how Richard, a film publicist, summed up his admiration.

"Hey, is this my funeral?" you asked.

You ordered a chocolate sundae for dessert. I took a tawny port. You smiled like a nitwit. Too much vodka followed by too much wine.

"Your turn, Frank."

"Speech! Speech!"

From inside your jacket pocket, you lifted out a piece of folded paper. I looked over your shoulder.

"What's that?" I whispered loudly. I didn't want you to make a fool of yourself. I wanted you to say a few words. I tugged on your shirt. "Frank," I pleaded, trying to get control of my breathing. In out, in out, in out.

You rose, shrugged a bit, smoothed the paper, and began.

"I thought I'd read you a list of names," you said.

You coughed a fake little cough and cleared your throat.

"Like?" Crystal shouted boisterously.

I slugged down the port and noted the nearest exit.

You ignored Crystal's question, sat down, and took a bite of ice cream.

Richard tried to peer over your shoulder, but you shoved the papers into your lap.

"You don't have to do anything," Harold said sheepishly.

"Right," Richard chimed. "We're here to have a good time."

"Good time," you sneered.

I stared at the pattern on the rug and patted the back of one hand with the other. I counted backwards from ten. Grounding, I think it's called.

"A toast!" Harold stood. Staggered and stood.

"To health!" I yelled exuberantly.

"Absolutely," everyone murmured except Crystal, too young to know there was nothing else more important.

Everyone clinked their glasses. Harold sat down.

When you started to rise again, I tugged again. And blinked three times which was always our signal that it was time to go.

You spoke softly and deliberately. "Honor the fallen for March," you said.

Spence A. McNeil	19	James R. Dillon Jr.	19
Jason Profitt	23	Brian Matthew Kennedy	25
Jay Thomas Aubin	36	Ryan Anthony Beaupre	30
Kendall Damon Waters-Bey	29	Therrel S. Childers	30
Jose Gutierrez	22	Brandon S. Tobler	19
Eric J. Orlowski	26	Nicolas M. Hodson	22
Thomas Mullen Adams	27	Christopher Scott Seifert	27
Brian Rory Buesing	20	Brendon C. Reiss	23
Michael J. Williams	31	Phillip A. Jordan	42
Jason Hicks	25	Jason Plite	21
John Stein	39	John Teal	29
Michael Maltz	42	Tamara Archuleta	23
Frederick E. Pokorney Jr	31	Randal Kent Rosacker	21
Thomas J. Slocum	22	Donald Ralph Walters	33
George Edward Buggs	31	Jonathan L. Gifford	30
Robert J. Dowdy	38	Ruben Estrella-Soto	18
James M. Kiehl	22	Patrick R. Nixon	21
Johnny Villareal Mata	35	Lori Ann Piestewa	23
Jamaal R. Addison	22	Howard Johnson II	21
Brandon Ulysses Sloan	19	Michael E. Bitz	31
David K. Fribley	26	Jose A. Garibay	21
Jorge A. Gonzalez	20	Tamario D. Burkett	21

You enunciated each name. You stated each age. No one knew what you meant. No one understood.

"Whoa!" Harold said, glancing at me nervously. An expression that said he didn't know it was this bad.

I watched either Crystal or the rug. She was working on a hangnail.

"Wait! I haven't finished!" you said. "Gregory Stone 40, Evan T. James 20, Jacob Frazier 24, Orlando Morales 33. . . ."

I interrupted, "Frank, honey, sit down."

You sat down and attacked your dessert. After a minute of silence, other pieces of folded papers fell from your jacket. You kneaded out the creases, sorted them in a stack, placed them in a pile beside your coffee cup. You had neatly typed them out. You held each page up like a flash card.

List of Dead Iraqi Civilians - March 2003

unknown	unknown	unknown	unknown	unknown
unknown	unknown	unknown	unknown	unknown
unknown	unknown	unknown	unknown	unknown
unknown	unknown	unknown	unknown	unknown
unknown	unknown	unknown	unknown	unknown
unknown	unknown	unknown	unknown	unknown
unknown	unknown	unknown	unknown	unknown
unknown	unknown	unknown	unknown	unknown
unknown	unknown	unknown	unknown	unknown
unknown	unknown	unknown	unknown	unknown
unknown	unknown	unknown	unknown	unknown
unknown	unknown	unknown	unknown	unknown
unknown	unknown	unknown	unknown	unknown
unknown	unknown	unknown	unknown	unknown
unknown	unknown	unknown	unknown	unknown
unknown	unknown	unknown	unknown	unknown
unknown	unknown	unknown	unknown	unknown
unknown	unknown	unknown	unknown	unknown
unknown	unknown	unknown	unknown	unknown
unknown	unknown	unknown	unknown	unknown
unknown	unknown	unknown	unknown	unknown
unknown	unknown	unknown	unknown	unknown
unknown	unknown	unknown	unknown	unknown
unknown	unknown	unknown	unknown	unknown
unknown	unknown	unknown	unknown	unknown
unknown	unknown	unknown	unknown	unknown
unknown	unknown	unknown	unknown	unknown
unknown	unknown	unknown	unknown	unknown
unknown	unknown	unknown	unknown	unknown
unknown	unknown	unknown	unknown	unknown
unknown	unknown	unknown	unknown	unknown
unknown	unknown	unknown	unknown	unknown
unknown	unknown	unknown	unknown	unknown
unknown	unknown	unknown	unknown	unknown
unknown	unknown	unknown	unknown	unknown
unknown	unknown	unknown	unknown	unknown
unknown	unknown	unknown	unknown	unknown
unknown	unknown	unknown	unknown	unknown
unknown	unknown	unknown	unknown	unknown
unknown	unknown	unknown	unknown	unknown
unknown	unknown	unknown	unknown	unknown
unknown	unknown	unknown	unknown	unknown
unknown	unknown	unknown	unknown	unknown
unknown	unknown	unknown	unknown	unknown
unknown	unknown	unknown	unknown	unknown

unknown	unknown	unknown	unknown	unknown
unknown	unknown	unknown	unknown	unknown
unknown	unknown	unknown	unknown	unknown
unknown	unknown	unknown	unknown	unknown
unknown	unknown	unknown	unknown	unknown
unknown	unknown	unknown	unknown	unknown
unknown	unknown	unknown	unknown	unknown
unknown	unknown	unknown	unknown	unknown
unknown	unknown	unknown	unknown	unknown
unknown	unknown	unknown	unknown	unknown
unknown	unknown	unknown	unknown	unknown
unknown	unknown	unknown	unknown	unknown
unknown	unknown	unknown	unknown	unknown
unknown	unknown	unknown	unknown	unknown
unknown	unknown	unknown	unknown	unknown
unknown	unknown	unknown	unknown	unknown
unknown	unknown	unknown	unknown	unknown
unknown	unknown	unknown	unknown	unknown
unknown	unknown	unknown	unknown	unknown
unknown	unknown	unknown	unknown	unknown
unknown	unknown	unknown	unknown	unknown
unknown	unknown	unknown	unknown	unknown
unknown	unknown	unknown	unknown	unknown
unknown	unknown	unknown	unknown	unknown
unknown	unknown	unknown	unknown	unknown
unknown	unknown	unknown	unknown	unknown
unknown	unknown	unknown	unknown	unknown
unknown	unknown	unknown	unknown	unknown
unknown	unknown	unknown	unknown	unknown
unknown	unknown	unknown	unknown	unknown
unknown	unknown	unknown	unknown	unknown
unknown	unknown	unknown	unknown	unknown
unknown	unknown	unknown	unknown	unknown
unknown	unknown	unknown	unknown	unknown
unknown	unknown	unknown	unknown	unknown
unknown	unknown	unknown	unknown	unknown
unknown	unknown	unknown	unknown	unknown
unknown	unknown	unknown	unknown	unknown
unknown	unknown	unknown	unknown	unknown
unknown	unknown	unknown	unknown	unknown

unknown unknown unknown unknown unknown
unknown unknown unknown unknown unknown
unknown unknown unknown unknown unknown
unknown unknown unknown unknown unknown
unknown unknown unknown unknown unknown
unknown unknown unknown unknown unknown
unknown unknown unknown unknown unknown
unknown unknown unknown unknown unknown
unknown unknown unknown unknown unknown
unknown unknown unknown unknown unknown
unknown unknown unknown unknown unknown
unknown unknown unknown unknown unknown
unknown unknown unknown unknown unknown
unknown unknown unknown unknown unknown
unknown unknown unknown unknown unknown
unknown unknown unknown unknown unknown
unknown unknown unknown unknown unknown
unknown unknown unknown unknown unknown
unknown unknown unknown unknown unknown
unknown unknown unknown unknown unknown
unknown unknown unknown unknown unknown
unknown unknown unknown unknown unknown
unknown unknown unknown unknown unknown
unknown unknown unknown unknown unknown
unknown unknown unknown unknown unknown
unknown unknown unknown unknown unknown
unknown unknown unknown unknown unknown
unknown unknown unknown unknown unknown
unknown unknown unknown unknown unknown
unknown unknown unknown unknown unknown
unknown unknown unknown unknown unknown
unknown unknown unknown unknown unknown
unknown unknown unknown unknown unknown
unknown unknown unknown unknown unknown
unknown unknown unknown unknown unknown
unknown unknown unknown unknown unknown
unknown unknown unknown unknown unknown
unknown unknown unknown unknown unknown
unknown unknown unknown unknown unknown
unknown unknown unknown unknown unknown
unknown unknown unknown unknown unknown
unknown unknown unknown unknown unknown

unknown	unknown	unknown	unknown	unknown
unknown	unknown	unknown	unknown	unknown
unknown	unknown	unknown	unknown	unknown
unknown	unknown	unknown	unknown	unknown
unknown	unknown	unknown	unknown	unknown
unknown	unknown	unknown	unknown	unknown
unknown	unknown	unknown	unknown	unknown
unknown	unknown	unknown	unknown	unknown
unknown	unknown	unknown	unknown	unknown
unknown	unknown	unknown	unknown	unknown
unknown	unknown	unknown	unknown	unknown
unknown	unknown	unknown	unknown	unknown
unknown	unknown	unknown	unknown	unknown
unknown	unknown	unknown	unknown	unknown
unknown	unknown	unknown	unknown	unknown
unknown	unknown	unknown	unknown	unknown
unknown	unknown	unknown	unknown	unknown
unknown	unknown	unknown	unknown	unknown
unknown	unknown	unknown	unknown	unknown
unknown	unknown	unknown	unknown	unknown
unknown	unknown	unknown	unknown	unknown
unknown	unknown	unknown	unknown	unknown
unknown	unknown	unknown	unknown	unknown
unknown	unknown	unknown	unknown	unknown
unknown	unknown	unknown	unknown	unknown
unknown	unknown	unknown	unknown	unknown
unknown	unknown	unknown	unknown	unknown
unknown	unknown	unknown	unknown	unknown
unknown	unknown	unknown	unknown	unknown
unknown	unknown	unknown	unknown	unknown
unknown	unknown	unknown	unknown	unknown
unknown	unknown	unknown	unknown	unknown
unknown	unknown	unknown	unknown	unknown
unknown	unknown	unknown	unknown	unknown
unknown	unknown	unknown	unknown	unknown
unknown	unknown	unknown	unknown	unknown
unknown	unknown	unknown	unknown	unknown
unknown	unknown	unknown	unknown	unknown
unknown	unknown	unknown	unknown	unknown
unknown	unknown	unknown	unknown	unknown
unknown	unknown	unknown	unknown	unknown

unknown	unknown	unknown	unknown	unknown
unknown	unknown	unknown	unknown	unknown
unknown	unknown	unknown	unknown	unknown
unknown	unknown	unknown	unknown	unknown
unknown	unknown	unknown	unknown	unknown
unknown	unknown	unknown	unknown	unknown
unknown	unknown	unknown	unknown	unknown
unknown	unknown	unknown	unknown	unknown
unknown	unknown	unknown	unknown	unknown
unknown	unknown	unknown	unknown	unknown
unknown	unknown	unknown	unknown	unknown
unknown	unknown	unknown	unknown	unknown
unknown	unknown	unknown	unknown	unknown
unknown	unknown	unknown	unknown	unknown
unknown	unknown	unknown	unknown	unknown
unknown	unknown	unknown	unknown	unknown
unknown	unknown	unknown	unknown	unknown
unknown	unknown	unknown	unknown	unknown
unknown	unknown	unknown	unknown	unknown
unknown	unknown	unknown	unknown	unknown
unknown	unknown	unknown	unknown	unknown
unknown	unknown	unknown	unknown	unknown
unknown	unknown	unknown	unknown	unknown
unknown	unknown	unknown	unknown	unknown
unknown	unknown	unknown	unknown	unknown
unknown	unknown	unknown	unknown	unknown
unknown	unknown	unknown	unknown	unknown
unknown	unknown	unknown	unknown	unknown
unknown	unknown	unknown	unknown	unknown
unknown	unknown	unknown	unknown	unknown
unknown	unknown	unknown	unknown	unknown
unknown	unknown	unknown	unknown	unknown
unknown	unknown	unknown	unknown	unknown
unknown	unknown	unknown	unknown	unknown
unknown	unknown	unknown	unknown	unknown
unknown	unknown	unknown	unknown	unknown
unknown	unknown	unknown	unknown	unknown
unknown	unknown	unknown	unknown	unknown
unknown	unknown	unknown	unknown	unknown
unknown	unknown	unknown	unknown	unknown

"So what was that?" Richard asked, suppressing his distaste.

You didn't answer. You looked at me, blinked three times, and rose to go.

Crystal rose with us.

"I really liked meeting you, Frank Teller," she said flirtatiously. She kissed him on the lips.

Then she turned and hugged me. "And you, too." I could feel her boobs and stiff pushup bra against my throat. Her hair smelled like honeydew.

"I liked *that*," she said to him and winked at me. "I like Harold's weird friends best of all."

A deep, committed laugh bubbled out of her mouth.

I was so grateful that I grabbed her.

You picked up my shawl and draped it tenderly around my shoulders. There were tears in your eyes. Richard, Harold, the others waved cheerfully as we stood by the table. We left without offering to pay our portion of the bill.

"What are the Bucks up to after all these years?" Kim asked.

"Same old," you said.

"Same old, same old?"

"The more things change, the more they stay the same."

"Then you had a good time?"

"I wouldn't go that far, would you?"

"No, I wouldn't go that far."

"But passable?"

"Harold had high expectations," you said.

"Which put a strain on everyone?"

"He wanted to impress his new girlfriend."

"She impressed us, wouldn't you say?"

"Nice?"

"Nice wasn't exactly the point."

"So she must have been the center of attention."

"Frank got a little attention. Didn't you, honey?"

"I'm going to bed."

"Good idea. Let's get an early start."

"I thought we'd go to Farmers' Market for beignets."

"Not this trip, Kim."

"Good-night, Frank."

"Was it awful?"

"Almost."

"You knew it would be."

"I thought it might give him a connection to something outside himself. The only thing that has distracted him from the illness is the war. I can't say that's a good thing."

"You're a good thing. Thank God, he has you."

"Simon used to say I was an angel but not a saint."

"You also took care of him. When he was strung out, you took care of him."

"I took care of him like a lover. I knew he would recover. I got something, too."

Part 3

Name of Staff Person
Department of Human Resources
Company Name
Address
City, CA Zip

Dear _____:

I agree with you and the palaver of local, national, and global corporations and multinationals that Human Resources are the richest resources.

Take a human being, for instance. He or she is born, for instance. If they are fortunate, they have loving parents. If they are fortunate, their country is not at war. If they are fortunate, there are means to provide them with shelter, wholesome food and clean water and air, clothing and shoes. If they are fortunate, there are free and decent schools. If they are fortunate, there is leisure time for them to play. If they are fortunate, their neighbors are caring and kind people. If they are fortunate, there are not too many dangers. There aren't any wild and hungry beasts. Or drug dealers and crime. Or brutal police. Or bombs, land mines, and hordes of foreign soldiers. Or incomprehensible political agendas that shatter family life.

A little about myself: I was fortunate. I grew up in Southern California. There were often storms in the winter, but for months, sometimes as long as May through November, it never rained. I was fortunate to have a house and plenty of food. I had a mother, a father, and a sister. My mother was a cold person, but eventually I learned not to blame myself. I played with my friends at the local park and in the street. I went to schools where I had a few inspiring teachers. I was on the track team. I was very good at hurdles. I had friends. We heard about wars, but they were always far away.

Free of care for my survival, I grew up. I went to top universities (see attached RESUME). I excelled. And what did I discover? I found out that I was a resource. Not to myself, or my loved ones, or my friends, but to you. For a bit of money my employer could take my mind, my creativity, almost all my energy, and much of my time. So to speak, I was one half of an exchange. A man for a _____? You fill in the blank.

That's what I haven't quite figured out. I know what you'll get if you hire me because I know myself. I know that I am a conscientious, industrious, reliable, and thoughtful man. If you hire me, you'll get nearly my entire being.

In exchange I need to have your assurance that it's worth it. Aside from the benefits -- medical and dental insurance, two weeks paid vacation per year, holidays, a retirement package, drug and alcohol abuse counseling -- what does your company offer its full-time employees?

I'd like to know that my eight to ten (or more) hours a day for five days a week with rotatations on weekends will add up to something worthy of remembering. I can say it was worth a legacy when they bury me at the end. If you can reassure me, I would very much like to work for you.

Thank you for your consideration. I look forward to hearing from you at your earliest convenience.

Yours sincerely,
Franklin Teller
506 Carmel Avenue
Albany, CA 94706
(510) 524-3088

Sometimes I hear phones ringing from other houses. I think they've made a mistake. I think the calls are for you and they dialed the wrong number. Sometimes I hear two phones at once, on either side of the house, ringing in different tones. I only know a few neighbors by name. They hardly know us. That's why someone put a hostile note on our car instead of knocking on the door, introducing himself, apologizing for the disturbance, and asking you to be more careful when you park on the street. That would have been a measure of civilized life. You said I should examine history to find out about the measures. But you never hear the phones. You say the voices in your head are louder than anything outside.

"Do you think we communicate well?"

[long pause]

"Did you hear me?"

"Yes."

"Is that your answer?"

"No."

"What's your answer?"

"We do not communicate well."

"Why?"

"The truth? I don't communicate with you at all."

[pause]

"Why is that?"

[pause]

"It's hard sometimes for you to follow a train of thought. If I'm honest, you get defensive. After I tell you private things, I overhear you repeating them to your sister."

"Like what?"

"I can't remember right now."

"Try."

[pause]

"When I try to talk about us, you say you can't formulate the right words from your thoughts."

"That's true."

"How are we supposed to speak about . . . difficult things?"

"I don't know."

"That's why I say there's no communication."

"I'm a terrible mate."

"That's exactly what I mean. You react and the subject completely changes. Now I have to assure you that you're not terrible."

"Thanks."

"Or shut up because I've made you feel bad."

"Worse."

"So what made you ask if we communicate well?"

[pause]

"I read something on the internet about the secrets of happy couples."

"You mean you hadn't noticed?"

Even if you're not feeling cheerful, pretend. You don't need to dump your shit everywhere. I'm sick of your bad moods, sick of being your pooper-scooper. That's all I am. Guess what? I want to see you smile in the morning before I head off to work. I don't care if you think it's hypocritical. Too bad.

Whether people actually change or life changes them is less important than the changes themselves. Everything changes. That's a law of Life. People want to believe in something that doesn't change. That's God. People want to believe in something that explains change. That's God. But you don't believe in God. Nevertheless, you want to believe you and I are immutable. If only we could accept change without blame.

Eight is the Magic Number for Happy Couples
by Suzy Lipton, M.S.W.

Happy couples will tell you that when the honeymoon is over, the real relationship begins. Join me to explore 8 things that happy couples like to do:

* *Cultivate common interests.* Common interests not only make you more interesting, but they keep you from appearing too independent.
* *Emphasize to yourself and others what your mate does right rather than wrong.* Accentuating the positive is an essential ingredient for happy couples.
* *Go to bed at the same time.* Resist going to bed at different times, even if you have to get up later to do something.
* *Whenever you leave for work, remember to tell your mate, "I love you!"* This will give your mate a high point at low points during the day.
* *At night, remember to say, "Sleep well!"* This reminds your mate that even after a disagreement, you care.
* *Hug each other at the end of the workday.* This guarantees that your bodies renew their closeness daily.
* *Walk hand in hand or side by side.* This shows that togetherness is more important than the journey.
* *Make sure to act proud of your partner.* Affectionate contact in public is a way of affirming to yourself and the world that you belong together.

These actions may not come naturally, but if you build them into your daily life, they will become a happy habit.

©Suzy Lipton is a professional best-selling authoress, co-editor of the forthcoming "Eight Secrets to Ensure a Forever Relationship," and co-founder of CouplesRU.com

Although you quit smoking the day of the stroke, there's an ashtray from Bix at the edge of your desk. "A reminder of fun," you say. There's also another prized possession, a Ronson silver tabletop lighter, companion to countless packs of unfiltered Camels. Behind the desk on the wall are photos from hiking trips in Mexico and the Andes, and a young photo of me, ten years before you met me when I was a willow.

Through the skylight over the desk, a few dark clouds move slowly across the bright moon. Your books, mostly on archeology and natural studies, fill the shelves of the wall. Mahler's Seventh is playing.

"So how is the book proposal coming along?" I ask.

You don't answer. Or look up. Maybe you're listening to the music.

"The book proposal?" I persist, taking a seat opposite the desk on a damaged Philippe Starck folding chair, another prized possession. It's the same thing I ask every weekend. My way of encouraging you to commit to a project. Something. Anything. *You aren't brain dead!* I yell inside my head.

I settle in, waiting. Waiting, I guess, to talk about the future. Not that I have any bright ideas. But I need reassurance that you have a future.

"Your book proposal?" One more time.

You heave the lighter at the floor where it ricochets and cuts my chin.

"Owwww!" you say feeling my pain.

I'm silent. Cold. Furious. I touch my chin and feel the blood. My fingers are smeared with it. It's quite a lot, I think, watching the drops splatter on my blouse and skirt.

"Laurie! You're cut!"

I say nothing.

"Laurie, I didn't mean to!"

Endless excuses for everything.

The blood puddles on my skirt. I don't even like the skirt. I won't wash or have it cleaned. I'll throw it away.

A Folding Chair by
Philippe Starck

Philippe Starck is something of a 1980s cult designer with an impressive track record: he designed the French presidential apartment at the Élysée Palace, the nightclub Les Bains Douches, as well as several American hotel chains. The appealing things about his chair is its simplicity, practicality, and elegance of line. It clearly looks back to PEL, or perhaps the Bauhaus and Gerrit Rietveld for its roots. It has the very real advantage of being practical for modern living and not expensive to produce.

I lie down in the backseat and keep my chin raised. There's a lot of blood, but it doesn't hurt. I haven't spoken yet except to tell you that the car key is next to the basket where we keep the mail. It's where we keep the keys, but you never remember.

"You okay back there?"

I grunt.

"We're almost there," you say, sounding cheerful.

I look through the back window at the neon signs for markets and the billboards advertising Chevy trucks.

"Is the ice helping?"

The car swerves onto the split freeway ramp, heading towards the Richmond-San Rafael Bridge.

"You made a mistake," I say, trying to be patient.

"I realize that. I'll get off at the next exit."

"Head up San Pablo Avenue and take a left on Barrett."

"I know."

The ER isn't crowded. You hold my arm while I hold the ice bag. We pass a guard and metal detector and enter a windowless room. Two TVs are perched in the corners, both turned to the Late Show, the sound mercifully off.

The receptionist glances at the blood on my blouse and skirt. Beverly is scripted on her plastic nametag and pinned to her blue smock.

"I'll do this," you say. "You sit down."

I feel weak. Not from loss of blood but the fatigue of life's nasty little surprises. I'd rather deal with a tragedy than a cut on my chin. I hate the bother.

"Name?" I hear Beverly ask you.

"Laurie, L-A-U-R-I-E," you say firmly but can go no further.

"Last name?"

I glance over. Your face is blank.

"Willits," I shout.

I hear you repeat our address and zip code. When Beverly asks for my insurance number, you turn back to me.

"W-994086," I say.

Beverly can hear me.

When she asks for my date of birth, you're off by a year. You can't answer my status on allergies to drugs. Or list of medications. Or my physician's name.

After the forms are stamped, they're shuffled into a box. There are three emergencies ahead of us.

You sit next to me. In the fluorescent light, the skin on your bare arm is onion white. Your face blotched with faint roseola marks. Your eyes small and dark. The dye in your hair faded to brown.

Across the room, an old woman sits cradling a young boy on her lap. The boy's eyes are closed, his chocolate skin chalky. He's not so young, maybe six or seven. And big for his age.

"Baby Glorious, baby Glorious," she croons. She has great raccoon rings under her eyes as if she hasn't slept for a very long time. She nods sympathetically at the blood on my clothes and pulls the child deeper into her large chest.

"Can I get you something?" you ask, jerking towards the vending machine.

At the moment, I want nothing from you, ever again.

"Maybe she wants a drink," I say.

You turn to the old woman. "Can I get you something?" you ask kindly.

She shakes her head and continues chanting, "Baby Glorious, Baby Glorious, Baby, Baby, Baby Glorious."

You put six quarters in the machine. The clunk of the can falling into the receptacle hurts my head.

"How will you say it happened?" you ask. There is sweat on your forehead and upper lip. Your breath smells like sawdust.

I haven't thought about it. "Accident," I say.

"Thank you," you whisper, taking my hand. "Thank you."

You say you should give it up.

You say, "I'm going to give it up."

At first, I think you mean you are going to give up, but when I ask you to repeat what you said, I hear "it."

It is a peculiar word because it can mean everything or nothing.

"Give up?" I almost don't dare ask.

You laugh in that bitter way I hate. "I've already given up."

"But give *it* up like what . . . renunciation?"

I'm thinking of sellers at the flea market who decided to get rid of everything they own. I admire them. Like them, I hate having so much. We all have too much. At least, the people I know. But why everything?

"Maybe," you say mysteriously which in your case is evasive.

"You mean me? You mean us?"

"No." You seem hurt.

Give it up, give it up? I mutter all day, trying to figure it out.

Your arms folded around me. I was encircled by your arms. They contained, protected, sheltered me. What a rare feeling. To feel contained and sheltered.

We're supposed to feel the Earth hold us up. We're supposed to feel we have a place between the sky and the ground. In college I took tai chi where they teach you that. I took six months of tai chi. A plumb line goes from the top of your head through the arches of your feet into the earth.

In dance class they also teach you that. I took a few modern dance classes. I liked it, but I couldn't manage with work. Then after your stroke, I couldn't manage anything.

Most of the time, I feel my shoes and legs are heavy when I stand too long. Or my back aches when I sit too long. But in the dream, I was light and you were holding me like a child. When I woke, I asked myself, *Who was that woman?*

You said I called out Simon's name in my sleep.

"Are you still in love with Simon?" you asked.

"No."

"I wouldn't blame you."

"No!"

"I've disappointed you."

I thought about the contentment of the dream and the mysterious woman.

I answered honestly, "I love you."

"But you called his name."

"Sometimes I dream about him. Sometimes the past seems easier than the present."

You nodded. You understood that.

"You say you don't love him?"

"I love him. I love everyone I ever loved."

You understood that, too.

"And you love me although I'm. . . ?" you asked, sounding childish. You couldn't find the word.

broken

It makes me happy to drive along the Embarcadero. It's a true esplanade (one of our favorite words). The water dancing on the shore. The distant hills of Marin. The humps of islands in the Bay. The majestic palms by the roadway. The liveliness of the Ferry Building. The colorful antique trolleys clacking on the tracks. We have the Loma Prieta earthquake to thank for this beauty. It takes a cataclysm of some kind, natural or manmade, to reverse certain horrors of progress. Some wanted to rebuild the damaged freeway, others fought to tear it down. Its destruction is one of the best things that has happened in my lifetime.

We left Jim's place at midnight. Bay Street was empty. The moon hung like a gold spangle over the city. I was happy, and you seemed so too after a couple of glasses of wine and the company of your old friend. But you worried me. No matter how peaceful and silent and innocuous the moment, you always worry me. On the way to the bridge, you insisted I drive around the corner and take Beale Street. You said you wanted to see the Bechtel building by moonlight.

When I found this on your desk, I got scared. I thought I shouldn't be snooping, but I need to know what you're up to. I need to know if you're planning something and haven't told me.

About the ICRC | ICRC activities | The ICRC worldwide | Focus | Humanitarian law | Info resources | News

Home > The ICRC worldwide > Middle East and North Africa > Iraq

Caught in the cross-fire: Baghdad
Vatche Arslanian (47), the ICRC's logistics coordinator in Iraq, was killed on 8 April when his vehicle was caught in cross-fire in Baghdad. Tributes were paid to him by relatives, colleagues and friends at a memorial ceremony in Geneva on 15 April.

The Vice-President of the Canadian Red Cross, **Ms. Kate Wood**, said Vatche -- Syrian-born of Armenian descent -- typified the spirit and core strengths of both Canada, his adopted country, and the International Red Cross & Red Crescent Movement. She spoke of his dedication and unabated commitment to community causes, including, since 1991, the Red Cross. Ms. Wood said that Vatche's friends and colleagues "will strive to promote respect for the emblems, so that others who follow in Vatche's footsteps will not do so in fear."

Two speakers recalled a radio interview given by Vatche after his first ICRC mission to Georgia in 2000, in which he said: *"Helping to bring a smile and dignity to a fellow human being is deeply fulfilling. It is the best reward that one can have and beats by far what one obtains from acquiring wealth, power and prestige. . . ."*

See **press release** 03/27 of 9 April 2003.
Read how Vatche described his job in Iraq in an **article** on this site.
See the tribute on the **Canadian Red Cross** website.

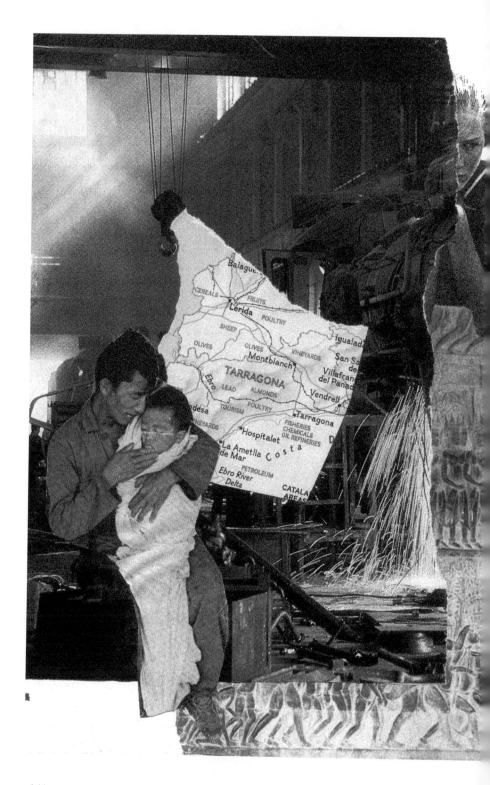

When I asked what you were doing today, you said you were going to work.

"What do you mean?"

"Exactly what I said."

"Did you find a job?"

"No, but I'm working at it."

I smiled. You smiled, too.

"I started a new diet," I said, biting into a dry English muffin.

"Are you fat?"

"You tell me."

"You don't look fat."

I started to blurt out that you wouldn't know, but I restrained myself. No blame, I repeated. No blame, no blame.

"Just a few pounds so I don't have to buy new pants."

You raised your eyebrow. "When I get my first paycheck, I'll take you shopping."

I put my face in my hands and started to cry.

"What's wrong?" you asked.

I pushed the plate aside. I wiped my eyes on a paper towel. I fluffed my hair.

"Nothing," I said, kissing you on the cheek. "Good luck with the job."

I know you went to San Francisco because I saw the BART ticket on the kitchen table. You said you went to check out Bechtel. I asked if you meant to apply for a job there. That would really shock me.

"You hate Bechtel," I said, thinking it's easier to hate entities (governments, corporations, armies) than deal with the frustrations of your own life. I have mixed feelings about hate. I think hate makes more hate.

"I have to take a stand," you said.

"That's hard to do," I said.

"It isn't a reason not to try."

"True," I said, guessing he was right. But I feel powerless. And when I look at Frank, he seems powerless, too.

"Anyway we aren't dropping the bombs. Or giving the orders. We aren't in control," you say.

"We pay taxes."

"We should stop paying taxes."

I asked what you did at Bechtel.

You said you walked around the building. You counted the windows on the front and sides. You counted the floors. You said the entire building was khaki-black.

"The color of death," you said.

You described the large pots of flowers, the begonias and ferns, next to the building. You said you walked back and forth under the portico, tapping each of the eleven pillars in front. A guard from the lobby finally came outside and asked what you were doing.

"Was he hostile?"

"No, just curious."

"What did you say?"

"Checking out Bechtel."

"Did he understand?"

"He shrugged and went back inside the lobby. He figured I was a nutcase from Market Street."

"Frank, he could have figured you were a terrorist. You could have gotten in trouble."

"Somewhat inept, wouldn't you say?"

"But suspicious."

"Maybe."

"He could have had you arrested."

"For?"

"Loitering! Isn't that what loitering means?"

"I didn't loiter long, but before I left. . . ."

"What? What!"

"I gave him a message for the CEO."

"You what?"

"A piece of paper."

"You wrote something?" I was alarmed.

"It was a slogan I wanted to share."

"What sort of slogan?"

"IF WE BOMB IT, BECHTEL REBUILDS IT!"

"Did you put down your name?"

"Frank for Bechtel Group, Inc."

"Frank!"

"I thought I should put my name in case they use it."

"They won't use it."

"It's rather cunning."

"Only from your point of view."

"But it has a ring of truth."

"I don't think that interests them."

When I asked about your projects for the week, you said you were going to do research on your book.

"Your book?" I was thrilled.

"I've got a bright idea now," you said.

"About?"

"About history and war: how the obliteration of the past dooms the future."

I pondered for a minute. It didn't sound very original.

"I want to write something that stirs. . . ."

You didn't finish.

"The imagination?" I tried.

"No, nothing imagined. I want people to get their hands around the past like it's tangible."

"That sounds good," I said.

"I thought so."

"You think it will be academic?"

"I hope not," you laughed.

"Are you going to write up a proposal?"

"After I get back, then I'll have something to put into a proposal."

"Back?"

"From Iraq," you said, looking out the window as if Iraq were across the street. I followed the direction of your head and looked, too.

"Are you crazy?"

"I guess so," you said, letting your eyes swim over to mine. We locked into each other.

"I think it's suicide."

"That's what I thought you'd think."

"I'm right, aren't I?"

"You want me to write a book. You and every other fucking person want me to find a fucking project. I have to leave the country to do research and you make this kind of accusation."

"What do you want me to do? Drive you to the airport?"

You made a twisted, apologetic smile. "Yes, I was thinking you might."

Rebuilding Iraq

USAID awarded the largest of its postwar Iraq contracts to Bechtel Group, Inc. April 17. The capital construction contract gives Bechtel an initial award of $34.6 million, but provides for funding of up to $680 million over 18 months subject to Congress' approval. Bechtel's primary activities under the contract will include rebuilding power generation facilities, electrical grids, water and sewage systems and airport facilities in Iraq. The company has said it plans to subcontract a number of these projects.

Bechtel Group, Inc., the San Francisco-based engineering company, has been in the construction business for more than 100 years and has completed close to 20,000 projects in 140 countries. The privately owned firm, which had revenues of $13.3 billion last year, has made a number of friends in Washington over the years. Former Secretary of State George Shultz, once Bechtel's president, now serves on the company's board of directors.

http://www.opensecrets.org/news

BECHTEL CORPORATION
ABOUT BECHTEL--VISION + VALUES

Vision

To be the world's premier engineering, construction, and project management company.

* Customers and partners will see us as integral to their success. We will anticipate their needs and deliver on every commitment we make.
* People will be proud to work at Bechtel. We will create opportunities to achieve the extraordinary, and we will reward success.
* Communities will regard us as responsible—and responsive. We will integrate global and local perspectives, promote sound management of resources, and contribute to a better quality of life.

Values

Building on a family heritage that spans more than 100 years, we will continue to be privately owned by active management and guided by firmly held values.

* Ethics. Uncompromising integrity, honesty, and fairness are at the heart of our company.
* Excellence. We set high standards. We apply advanced technology, and we continually innovate and improve. We thrive on challenge and accomplishment.
* Fair Return. We earn a return that fairly rewards the value we deliver.
* Mutual Respect. We work by our Leadership Covenants, which encourage openness, teamwork, and trust. We value an inclusive culture based on diverse background, experience, and views.
* Safety. Zero accidents is our unwavering goal—people's lives depend on it.
* Sustainability. We plan and act for the future—for the long-term good of our company, our customers, and our world.

http://www.bechtel.com/visionvalues.htm

Decades after the Vietnam War ended, TV pundits in laundered shirts and silk ties calmly compare this war to that, causally discussing the carnage. I can see how it drives you crazy.

"The waste of the effort. . . ."
"That killed tens of thousands of Americans. . . ."
"And millions of Vietnamese. . . ."
"And destroyed a country. . . ."
"And poisoned the water and land. . . ."

Some were in government then. Some at the Pentagon. Some gave orders. Some followed orders. They were insiders. They knew. You predict that's what they will be saying in the future. Ten, twenty, thirty years from now. In neckties and pressed shirts, they will speak of the devastation of Iraq and how the ravaged lives and wasted dollars weren't worth it.

From *Inanna* you tore out page 4:

> *In the first days, in the very first days,*
> *In the first nights, in the very first nights,*
> *In the first years, in the very first years,*
>
> *In the first days when everything needed was brought into being,*
> *In the first days when everything needed was properly nourished,*
> *When bread was baked in the shrines of the land,*
> *And bread was tasted in the homes of the land,*
> *When heaven had moved away from earth,*
> *And earth had separated from heaven,*
> *And the name of man was fixed. . . .*

Dear Frankie,

Enclosed is a check for your trip. It should come in handy although once you get over there, things will be VERY cheap. I went to Egypt just after the war. I love Egypt. Promise me, you'll try to get out to the monastery in the Sinai. It's called St. Catherine's. You don't want to miss it.

I think it's tremendous you're going off on an adventure. Best thing for you. You'll pick up plenty of material for a book. Take some fatherly advice: don't pick up anything else.

Jess tells me Laurie is worried about your safety. Jess is worried. But I say: let the women worry. That's what they're good at.

I love Cairo. Wish I could have traveled all over there, but it was a mess. I guess it's still a mess. But you and me, we're smart. We know how to stay out of a trouble and you're a whole lot smarter than I am.

Did I ever tell you I found out your IQ? I persuaded your 7th grade teacher to tell me. Well, I won't tell you. It might go to your head. Ha! Ha!

Anyway keep your wits about you. Don't spend this all at once. Most of all have a little fun.

Love, Dad

Your sister agrees it's a bad idea. For once we agree. Jess told me your father supports it. You never mentioned that. She said he even sent you money. You don't tell me anything. You say you don't want to upset me. UPSET ME? I'm more upset than I've ever been in my life. Jess said she doesn't respect people who do the right thing only to get attention. But I don't see how that applies to you. You aren't trying to get attention. Anyway, why is this the "right" thing?

Found on your desk:

Courage has no moral value in itself, for courage is not, in itself, a moral virtue. Vicious scoundrels, murderers, terrorists, may be brave. To describe courage as a virtue, we need an adjective: We speak of 'moral courage' — because there is such a thing as amoral courage, too. And resistance has no value in itself. It is the content of the resistance that determines its merit, its moral necessity. There is nothing inherently superior about resistance. All our claims for the righteousness of resistance rest on the rightness of the claim that the resisters are acting in the name of justice. And the justice of the cause does not depend on, and is not enhanced by, the virtue of those who make the assertion. It depends first and last on the truth of a description of a state of affairs that is, truly, unjust and unnecessary.

—Susan Sontag

HiLoTravel.com

A BRAVVI Company / 12326 San Pablo Avenue / Richmond, CA 94802

SALES PERSON: ZA   ITINERARY   DATE: 23 JUL

CUSTOMER NBR: 8659000   NKTLEO   PAGE: 01

    TO: FRANKLIN TELLER

        506 CARMEL AVE

        ALBANY CA 94706

        510-524-3088

        NKTLEO PRIORITY OVERNIGHT FEDEX

FOR: TELLER/FRANKLIN

23 JUL 03 - WEDNESDAY

  AIR   KLM ROYAL DUTCH   FLT:606   ECONOMY MULTI MEALS   LV SAN FRANCISCO

400P EQP: MD-11   DEPART: INTERNATIONAL TERMINAL   10HR 35MIN

24 JUL 03 - THURSDAY   1135A   NON-STOP

      AR AMSTERDAM   REF: 6LPC6Q

  AIR   KLM ROYAL DUTCH   FLT: 405   ECONOMY MULTI MEALS

      LV AMSTERDAM   715P EQP: BOEING 737   04HR 35MIN

25 JUL 03 - FRIDAY

      AR AMMAN   1250A   NON-STOP

      ARRIVE: NORTH TERMINAL   REF: 6LPC6Q

"You're a good man," I say.

You ask what I mean.

I'm crying. I can't speak. I want to get hold of myself, but I can't. I go into the bathroom to wash my face. I look at the mirror over the sink. I look turned inside out. Raw and swollen like an infected membrane. I am terrified.

"Why not Mexico?" I suggested weeks ago. "Surely, you can write a book about Mexico."

You said Mexico wasn't on your mind.

"If you were there, it would get into your mind. It would stimulate you. It's nearby, and you could come home easily."

"I can come home easily from anywhere in the world."

"Frank, please. What if you have another stroke?"

"You said I was a good man. What did you mean?"

"Good to put up with me, I guess."

"I like putting up with you."

"Then don't go," I sob.

You don't say anything to reassure me.

"Couldn't you change your mind?" I ask feebly like a child.

"I could."

"But will you, Frank? Will you for me?" That's my last card. It feels like a trick.

"Laurie." You put your hand on the back of my neck.

I'm sobbing again.

"Laurie," you whisper, sweeping me into your arms.

If you listen to classical music on the radio, you expect to find music that soothes you. I know this because I've listened to their ads. But they lie. There's a reason I never listen to classical music. It's too active. Too bright. Filled with too many passions that I don't understand. In the days before you left, you listened only to Mahler. After you were gone, I tried to uncover what you heard inside that music. Blood is what I heard. The music asked a thousand questions without one answer. It marched along, and the only relief were a few strings. I put your Mahler in the trash.

LJW

My dearest Frank —

I wrote this as soon as I got home
I wanted it to reach you as soon as possible
as soon as you touch ground in that place
whose name I can't bear to say

Since I dropped you off
not much has happened
I had an uneventful drive home
there was light traffic on the bridge
our neighbor came over to ask
if I'd sign a petition about library cuts
I started to say something about
the government spending on war
that's something you would say
but I decided not to discuss it
I signed the petition for both of us
later I was ashamed I didn't speak up

I read the quote from Susan Sontag on your desk
I think you possess moral courage
I'm sorry I made it hard for you to leave
I know you understand how scared I am
I don't want anything bad to happen to you
I never want anything bad to happen to you
those are selfish but loving reasons

hurrying to PO to get this in mail
I love you and will write again soon
Laurie

Found in your desk drawer:

Iraq Peace Team

Since September 2002, seasoned nonviolent activists have been on the ground in Iraq working in tandem with those in the United States and the world who seek to prevent a U.S. attack on Iraq. Initiated by <u>Voices in the Wilderness</u>, Iraq Peace Team will remain in Iraq in the event of an attack with these intentions:

--We will live among the Iraqi people during any aggression directed at them, including continued economic sanctions.
--We will use our presence and non-violent actions to witness, understand and expose the situation of both the civilian population of Iraq and highlight the importance of facilities such as water purification plants that are critical to daily life.
--We will report on our experiences in Iraq through this website, our support teams, and all who will listen.

Iraq Peace Team is not affiliated with Human Shield projects. Though we hope to remain in Iraq in the event of an attack, we don't consider ourselves "human shields." IPT exists to stand in solidarity with the people of Iraq. Voice in the Wilderness refuses to incorporate military language or ideas to describe the peace witness of IPT members.

Please check in often and get involved in whatever way you can. Your voice is needed to say "No!" to continued US attacks on Iraq.

IPT/Voices in the Wilderness contact info:
Tel: (773) 784-8065 Fax: (773) 784-8837 e-mail: <u>info@vitw.org</u>

LJW

My dearest Frank —

Today I went to a protest
outside the Berkeley BART station
I heard about it from Jess
but she didn't show up
I didn't know anybody
all the women were wearing black
no one said hello
only one smiled (a little) when I walked up
they were serious, really serious
and silent, holding signs
I stood by their side
wishing you could see me

All my love, L

The roses are in their second bloom. That's the only nice thing in the garden. David Austin's "Pilgrim" is bursting. It smells like lemon candy. I'll pick one, press it, and send it. Do you think it'll get through? I read about a man in jail who ate the flower that his wife brought him. Do you think they'd let me mail you a flower? Do I sound strange? I think I'm depressed. Now that you're gone, my depression has taken the place of yours. I pray you're all right. I actually pray. I get down on the floor on my knees and fold my hands like my mommy taught me.

Makehimbeallright Makehimbeallright
Makehimbeallright Makehimbeallright
Makehimbeallright Makehimbeallright
Makehimbeallright Makehimbeallright
Makehimbeallright Makehimbeallright
Makehimbeallright Makehimbeallright
Makehimbeallright Makehimbeallright
Makehimbeallright Makehimbeallright

Main Identity_____
From: "Frank Teller" <frankteller@earthlink.net>
To: "Laurie Willits" <ljw@pacbell.com>

Subject: THEY

> *They create a desolation*
> *And call it peace.*
> —Tacitus

LJW

My dearest Frank
I looked up Tacitus
now trying to read the Agricola
you'll make a smart person of me yet

War makes me sad, all of it makes me sad
your deciding to postpone your return
makes me saddest of all

I like writing more than email
then I can imagine you holding
something I wrote in your hand

I can't figure out why I keep this job
o yes I traded life for a pension
which sounds like something
you would say

last Friday I went back to the protest
this time I wore black
two women acknowledged me
they smiled which was a big relief

your dad called to chat
you'd better drop him a note
he says his letter was returned
now he's worried and wants to know
what I'm doing to get you home
I think I'll strangle him

in the meantime sending all my love,
Laurie

From the *Agricola* by Tacitus (circa 98 A.D.):

. . . Battles against Rome have been lost and won before; but hope was never abandoned, since we were always here in reserve. We, the choicest flower of Britain's manhood, were hidden away in her most secret places. Out of sight of subject shores, we kept even our eyes free from the defilement of tyranny. We, the most distant dwellers upon earth, the last of the free, have been shielded till today by our very remoteness and by the obscurity in which it has shrouded our name. Now, the farthest bounds of Britain lie open to our enemies; and what men know nothing about they always assume to be a valuable prize. But there are no more nations beyond us; nothing is there but waves and rocks, and the Romans, more deadly still than these—for in them is an arrogance which no submission or good behaviour can escape. Pillagers of the world, they have exhausted the land by their indiscriminate plunder, and now they ransack the sea. A rich enemy excites their cupidity; a poor one, their lust for power. East and West alike have failed to satisfy them. They are the only people on earth to whose covetousness both riches and poverty are equally tempting. To robbery, butchery, and rapine, they give the lying name of "government"; *they create a desolation and call it peace.*

—trans. from Latin by S.A. Handford
Penguin Books, 1948

Alternate translation: *they make a desert and call it peace.*

avocado
dish soap
peanuts
tortillas
cream cheese
oregano

call DDS

Main Identity_____
From: "Frank Teller" <frankteller@earthlink.net>
To: "Laurie Willits" <ljw@pacbell.com>
Subject: BOOM

The river isn't red, the sun rises every morning. Imagination makes
things worse but in this case, it is worse. But because I'm *in* it, it's easier
to handle. There's the reality of a real place rather than *my* reality.
However, it's absolutely grotesque. I don't have to imagine anymore.
As I write this, I can smell dust and blood. Rockets explode in the near
distance, the city covered in chemical fog. Sometimes there's potable
water. Rarely electricity. It's hotter than Hades. The ice cream parlors
are where we go to cool off. Noise unrelenting. Tanks and trucks
rumble through streets. It's an earthquake that lasts all day and night.
Impossible to think or sleep. I constantly believe I'm being shot but
strange to say it's moments of silence that terrify me more. From inside
the houses, women and children cry like kittens. And the men, it's clear
that I can't call myself their brother. I may never be their brother. I see
that brotherhood was my illusion. Nonetheless, I feel needed and have
decided to extend my stay.

Always, FT

LJW

Sounds like hospital work is rewarding
painful but rewarding
you sound better, stronger
I'm the reverse, scared of night noises
strange phones ring & dogs bark
your knee better? that's good
I hardly dare to ask but
when will you return?

Yours always, L

I took a walk at the marina. The water looked like cat eyes, the waves like melting glass. Is this the end of the world? I kept thinking about our first trip to Mexico, the pewter cup you bought me. I took it as a sign of our domestic happiness. More than a sign, perhaps a guarantee.

Found in your desk drawer:

Job opportunities at the ICRC: How to apply

Kindly send us your complete application in English or French, which should include:
- your CV
- copies of your diplomas
- copies of your work certificates
- **a personal history form and its appendix** (to print the form, see below)
- a one full-page description, in your own handwriting, of the reasons you would like to work for the ICRC.

Send all of the above to the following address:

INTERNATIONAL COMMITTEE OF THE RED CROSS
Recruitment Unit
19, av. de la Paix 1
CH - 1202 Genève

Candidates who **meet all the criteria** required for the position in question, and who submit **all the requested documents**, will be at an advantage.

While applications from people of any nationality will be taken into consideration, non-Swiss personnel are recruited on the basis of the agreements drawn up with the Red Cross or Red Crescent National Societies of their home country.

Print the **personal history form: Word format** or **PDF format**

Other documents in this section:
About the ICRC > Human resources

In other sections:
About the ICRC\Human resources\Skills always in demand
About the ICRC\Human resources\Vacancies

< Back to previous page

You shared nothing with me, Frank. NOTHING!

I wish I could say what's really on my mind. The longer you stay away, the more I believe you won't return. Maybe that's the depression. I wake up in the middle of the night and feel your death, the way I did when you were first sick. It's a smell that no breeze can blow away. Or incense mask. It stays. And stays. In the morning it's the same. A stale smell. Even when I get your notes, I believe they're teasing me, trying to convince me you're still alive. When the phone rings, I jump. I just wish the worst were over. The call will come tomorrow or later today, telling me you're dead. They'll say you were killed just after the email was sent. There's a hole in my stomach. That's where I feel the emptiness. I get up, brush my teeth, get dressed, go to work. The hole follows me. I wonder if you left because of me. I tried, Frank. I wish I could have done more than try.

To console myself, I think of things that you and I can do together when you come home. It's a helpful exercise. Maybe we'll learn to play bridge. Or go hiking in Wales. Isn't that what happy couples do? Cultivate common interests? Sometimes I wish I could live in the mountains and raise goats. I'm silly, yes? Daydreams, we used to call them. There's one more thing. If we had a child and you died, at least I'd have a piece of you.

Main Identity_____
From: "Laurie Willits" <ljw@pacbell.com>
To: "Frank Teller" <frankteller@earthlink.net>
Subject: Location

I tried calling your hotel.
They said you'd gone off for a couple of days.
They couldn't tell me where.
Baghdad is bad enough but to think you might be driving around.
Why don't you let me know these things? Why? Why? Why?

Main Identity_____

From: "Laurie Willits" <ljw@pacbell.com>
To: "Frank Teller" <frankteller@earthlink.net>
Subject: Freaking out

WHERE IN THE WORLD ARE YOU?

Main Identity_____

From: "Laurie Willits" <ljw@pacbell.com>
To: "Frank Teller" <frankteller@earthlink.net>
Subject: Location

It was a relief to talk. I was so SCARED. I didn't go to work for 2 days. Ever since you got sick, I've understood how important your feelings are, especially your feelings about yourself. But without you here, it's amazing how my own feelings come pouring out.

I went to Mountain View cemetery and took the tour. I thought it might help to have some pieces in place in case it comes to that. At first, I tried to talk myself out of having morbid thoughts, but I think it's better to let them drag me around. I think anyone would love to be buried there. An historical landmark with beautiful mausoleums, marble angels, large trees, a bird sanctuary, and tranquil park. For a few thousand dollars, if it comes to that, I can buy you a spot overlooking the Bay, and it's close enough to visit every day.

Behind every great fortune lies a great crime. Isn't that one of your favorite quotes? There are filthy rich families buried at Mountain View. Warren Bechtel (1872-1933) & Stephen Bechtel (1900-1989) are buried there. I know you don't want to be near them. But the place I have in mind isn't too near. It's at the top of a hill. I guess you must think I'm morbid. I guess that's what I am. I have to face the worst because it helps.

Every Friday I now stand with Women in Black. I've begun to understand the power of standing. Once we marched down Market Street, covered by these giant heads and holding giant baby corpses. I like the women who come. They're in mourning for the world, at least a few hours a week. They're committed and strong. I want to be like them. When I told them you were in Iraq trying to help, working at a hospital and distributing food, I guess it elevated their opinion of me. They hardly know anyone with your level of commitment. No one does.

Women in Black is on the Homeland Security Watch List! Are you?

I'm thinking when you come back, I'll go off. The boss said I could take a leave. I'd like to practice my Spanish so Mexico sounds appealing. Now that you've been alone, I mean not alone but without me, I think you'll be fine at home. I know you don't believe it, but I believe it. It will break the cycle. Our cycle. You go, then I go. Maybe after that, it can feel like a true new beginning.

Main Identity_____

From: "Frank Teller" <frankteller@earthlink.net>

To: "Laurie Willits" <ljw@pacbell.com>

Subject: ETA

customs in Chicago w/2 hr layover
ck ETA until then all my love Frank

Main Identity_____

From: "Laurie Willits" <ljw@pacbell.com>

To: "Frank Teller" <frankteller@earthlink.net>

Subject:

I hope you understand if I'm not there to pick you up

I made reservation for East Bay shuttle on Wed

they'll stop in front of UNITED terminal

go out front door, cross over to island

you'll find house key under pink geranium

cash under geranium in case you need to pay shuttle

fridge crammed w/food

I'm not far, only Inverness

need a little time to collect myself

TEL # in kitchen in case of emergencies

I promise I'll come home soon

I love you, L

LJW

Dearest Frank,

Maybe I'm doing this to punish you. I think that's part of it. Letting you know how it feels. When you were gone, it felt like punishment.

Or maybe I'm punishing myself for making it difficult for you. And prolonging some of the decisions we still have to make.

I know I need to sleep. I haven't slept since you left. At least, not without a couple of drinks. Me drinking? I bet that shocks you. Knowing you're home, I'll sleep.

I love you, L

The phone is ringing. It could only be you. I'm not answering. Although it could be the wrong number, still I won't answer. Anyway you don't know if I'm here. I could have gone to town. I could be at the beach. There's no answering machine so it rings and rings. Almost no phone does that anymore except the ones I used to hear in our neighborhood. If it isn't the wrong number, you'll probably call back. After dark when you think I'm here. Or even if it is the wrong number, the mistaken person may try again. I have no way of knowing unless I pick it up.

"Hello," you say.

I don't reply.

"Laurie?"

I don't reply.

"Laurie, is it you?"

"Yeah." [resentful]

"I just thought. . . ."

"Is there an emergency?"

"Isn't there always?" [laughing]

"I said only to call if there's an emergency." [reprimanding]

"Okay." [sheepish]

"Well, what is it?"

"I know I shouldn't impose." [apologizing]

"No, you shouldn't."

"Shall I hang up?"

"Tell me what you want, then we'll hang up."

"I just want you to. . . ." [stumbling]

Silence.

"I want you to know I could never have."

I hear you choke.

"And if I made your life more difficult, I want you to know. . . ."

"Oh, Frank," I cry.

"I understand you need to do what you need to. I respect that."

"I'm so relieved you're okay."

"Are you?"

"Of course, how could you doubt it?"

"I never did, but when you didn't want to meet me."

"*Want* isn't the right word."

"Sickness makes you selfish. For months all I've thought of is myself."

"I understood."

"More than understood, you've been so good."

"Not really."

"Better than I could have been."

We laugh because it's true.

"No pressure but I can hardly wait."

I smile into the phone.

"I think you'll be surprised."

"I don't like surprises."

"Well, surprised and unsurprised."

"Recently, I've had too many surprises."

"I know, but this is good, I promise."

When I hang up, everything has lifted. My heart feels light. My body feels young. I go to the beach and run five miles. I'm filled with exhilaration. And then I have a terrible thought: this terrible war saved us. A catastrophe of vast waste and profound suffering saved us. Suffering that you took on as your own. I changed because of what you did. We changed. But it's change extracted from a tragedy of massive proportions. It's not what I would have asked. Never from you or anyone. It feels like a crime. Yet here we are, together.

THE SOFT ROOM

Someone had a dream about me
last night   we were in a boat
in the desert   marooned for
several hours   it's not clear
to me now   my only certainty
is that I came to this person
in a dream   and our bodies
made light in a soft room

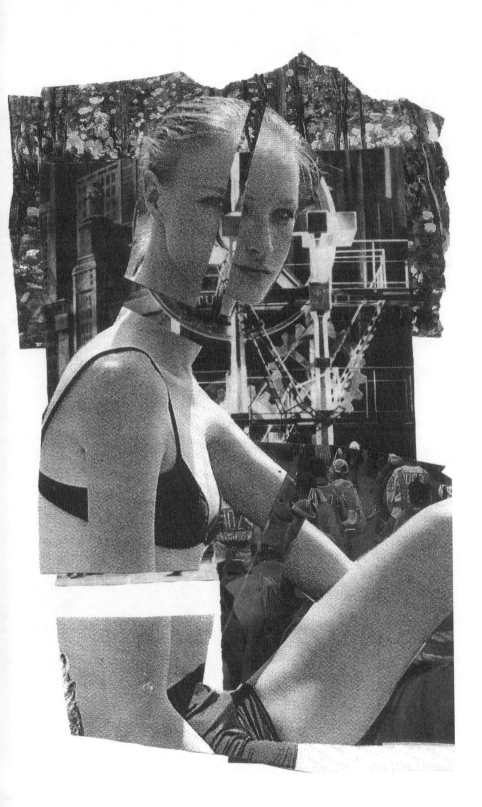

BUTTONS AND BLADES

Annie lived in a rundown adobe house in the middle of the bosque. She lived with a dozen other friends. They grew their own food and sometimes killed a chicken or a goat. The problem with the crops was they ripened at the same time. Hundreds of radishes, hundreds of zucchini. Too many to eat or give away so the rest were left to rot in the field. Somehow they never tired of Dede Lee's dish of shredding and sauteing zucchini with cheese, sitting under the pergola, watching the monsoons drench the mesas and the *virgas* fall through the distant purple sky.

Martin took off his pants and lay down. Annie put her mouth on him, holding him lightly with her lips until he got hard, squeezing her buttocks together and pressing the bell between her legs until a stream of melon juice spouted out of him and ran down her chin. He climbed into her, and they began to buck like rodeo bronco and rider, her fingers kneading, digging, pinching. Everything working to rise harder and faster, slipping down, up, down, up again to reach the summit where they both disappeared from their finite mortal bodies into a millisecond of the infinite.

Hey, let's get up.

Let's get dressed.

Let's wait until later.

Let's smoke a joint.

Let's change the sheets.

Let's water the plants.

Let's eat.

Let's get in the car.

Let's drink a beer.

Let's fuck.

Her bedroom walls were covered with blue toile printed with naked cherubs. And curtains and a bedspread to match. She searched between the tiny cherub legs to get an idea what was there. When her mother explained about babies, demonstrating with her fingers and thumb how a penis penetrated a vagina, Annie shrank into the floor. The mechanics were beyond her scope of comprehension. What she wanted to know was why it was called lovemaking. And if it hurt. And when it would happen. And why dark hairs were coming out her body in a place she was told not to touch. And would the hair continue to grow if she were good. . . .

The buttons were round and smooth. They came in different colors, sizes, and shapes. Bone, wood, plastic, shell. How things fastened. How parts connected. How people dressed and undressed. How buttons went into buttonholes. How her legs buttoned the mystery of the smooth good feeling. Buttons. Buttocks. Butter. Bum. Bun. Butt. Ivory. Tusks. Teeth. Horn. Cone. Needle. Thread. Thimble. Prick. Pick. Pluck. Screw. Winch. Nail. Sail. Bale. Batch. Latch.

When she was a child, she showered with her father. Standing beneath his elaborate jungle of hair. A wonder of protrusions. The water dropping from him onto her small shoulders. The man was a centaur.

I wish I could know the dick of an angel. That's what she wished. If she could. If she was supposed to. If it was all right. The way it felt so good when she was wearing a skirt and straddling a heater. Or pants whose seams perfectly fitted hers so she could drive and ride at the same time.

In school they'd ask how it would feel to slide down a razor blade. Everyone hated to hear that. They'd say, *Please don't say it again!* But someone would say it. Again and again. And she'd imagine it. The intensity of the pain thrilled her. The rush to escape thrilled her.

She carried her button secretly. As if she were a bird or a cloud or a fish. With a button buried in its center. And when her mother took her to shop and her father looked at her choices, she pointed to the buttons. And said they were the part she liked best.

OLD STUFF

Few could compete with the Chevy Nomad for design. In great shape for her age, considering she'd knocked around for twenty years: no dents, low mileage, classic GM lines with a robust V-8, two-tone turquoise and white, and very little rust. Tires and brakes were fine. AM radio worked. No rips in the vinyl upholstery. She only needed a valve job.

It was four in the afternoon when they cruised past the officials in Juarez into Mexico. They drove slowly as buses raced past, barreling down the broken highway, bouncing over the cracks in the asphalt, and occasionally hitting a cow. Most livestock stayed behind the barbed wire, although a few were tempted by roadside weeds. One step too far and driver, passengers, animal ended up crushed or dead.

Shacks multiplied, land flattened. Dry, dusty, monotonous Sonora. Martin was sleepy, and Annie suggested she drive. He said he could go a while longer. She scrunched beside him, her palm on his thigh. A message that she was glad to be with him and on the road. He held her hand, and to the rhythm of the moving car, they rubbed his jeans. She juggled his balls through the denim. He put his fingers down her shirt inside her bra, twisting her nipple and clamping her breast, stroking her sticky underwear. She swooned against the seat, then buried her head between his legs, exhaling over the cloth, blowing and chewing his jeans. The temperature rising until her face burned.

Everywhere there were offers to buy their car. But it was illegal to sell a foreign vehicle in Mexico. After Martin's cousin totaled his Corvette outside Los Mochis, he was jailed at the border for trying to enter California without his car. A double disaster.

Desert turned into mountain. Cooler and damper. At Durango they turned right and headed west, driving all night along the switchback road known as Devil's Spine.

STY IN THE EYE

A few years ago it was Paul in the backseat with Annie, returning from a dinner party at the Island Hotel in Cedar Key, famous for its hearts-of-palm salad. The car was big, comfortable, fast, all American. Friends were in the front. Everyone was a little drunk, a little high.

She lay her head in Paul's lap and unzipped his pants. She held the tip of him inside her mouth and did nothing else. They just enjoyed the speed of the car and the breeze of Florida's thick air.

She'd done nearly everything. Dry humping her way in and out of romances. But she waited to go all the way. She didn't want someone to possess a piece of her. She worried it might turn into a trophy. Or a ring. Or a chain. The next year she surrendered her cherry in a hotel room. Ready and relieved. Unburdened of virginity.

Get out of here! Get away from me! Leave me alone!

Paul shook her.

Wake up, Annie! You're dreaming!

But it wasn't a dream. She lay on the sofa, beating a pillow and going crazy, waiting for word. Dead or alive? Alive or dead?

"We found him," her uncle said.

He'd locked himself in a garage and let the motor run. The letters had already come that morning. Financial details for her mother. A loving apology to her. Dear Annie. Dear Whom It May Concern. Dear Nobody. Dear No One. Dear God. Dear Gone.

Her girlfriends adored him. He was a sweetheart to them all. When Suzanne was sixteen and got caught sleeping with Bobby Bergman, he said, "So what?" He loved the losers she brought home. The ones saying that their future could shove it up their ass. Now he was dead.

The ride to the cemetery in the black limos, the short service at the grave, the intense heat, the scent of perfume and magnolia, the Kaddish. She never wanted to see that place again.

But afterwards, he wouldn't stop haunting her. Infernal Daddy dreams. Bloody Daddy orgies. Daddy dives in every orifice. Daddy deadness.

Wake up, Annie! You're dreaming!

VENI, VIDI, VICI

If she could tell you how it feels when it's riding you up to the sky, and your whole body is condensed in a point and rockets away from you on waves. Something about the ocean: the motion, the smell, the origin. She has a theory about orgasm. About the feeling that turns you inside out. She thinks it came from the explosion of sperm pummeling the plasma membrane of an ovum. Pure fusion! Meaning since conception, everyone has been intimate with the most profound creative experience. And people who are isolated from life, maybe that's what they're most isolated from.

If she could make love once a week awesomely, it would be enough. But when someone is around, someone she loves, she yearns for contact. More and more she yearns. And coming doesn't matter. Not until the full moon when yearning escalates into hunger, and she knows that when someone touches her, anywhere or everywhere, she'll quake.

Social norms make women shy. Or they used to. Even bold women often have to overcome shyness. Reports that women's sexuality peaks at thirty has to do with the time it takes to overcome timidity. It never happened with her first lover. A decade older and a ladies' man, as handsome as Belmondo, he couldn't reach her. He knew it. He could tell she was faking. He blamed her. She blamed herself.

Last year she saw a man at a party. They didn't meet, but she asked his name and got his number. She called and invited him for coffee. The anxiety was grueling. He didn't remember her. He wasn't interested in coffee. But it was a useful exercise. She could understand what men constantly went through: see a girl, make a date, hope to get laid. A ritual that drives them to extract compensation for their humiliation. Everybody knows the rules. He spent the money so he can expect her to submit. Maybe she wants to submit. Or doesn't care. Or maybe he's a brute who forces her. Or begs her. There's humiliation on both sides.

She used to be a passive lover. Henry T. helped her get over that.

Whenever he came by, she put on a full slip and stiletto heels. They'd dance. Cheek to cheek. Bone to bone. Slow grind to salsa. There were steps for herself, steps for him, and steps when she couldn't tell the difference.

Annie likes to hover at the top of the wave. Suspended together, breathing together, connected by a stick and a hole. If she concentrates, she can feel that it's *her* penis. She can be both sexes at the same time. Outside in, inside out.

Kissing is her favorite part. Then and now. The original safe sex. It started in sixth grade at movie matinees and spread to parked cars and golf courses. The conjunction of soft tissue. The center of breath, speech, and nourishment. Opening on opening. Face on face. Skin on skin. Specificity of lips, tongue, gums. Wet, dry, rough, smooth, whiskered. Raindrops and tsunamis. Some withholding, others charging. A telegraph of an entire personality in a kiss!

THE ISLAND

Annie skipped past the ruffle of sea, waded in and floated on her back, fluttering her arms to keep from sinking. In the azure *agua* she felt clean and salty. The clear Caribbean with its white sandy bottom. Forget about the cliff on the far side of the island where garbage was thrown into the water.

Martin dog-paddled to her floating body. He licked the water off her waist. He took her fingers and crammed them in his mouth. He sucked each knuckle and slurped her wrists. He grabbed her hair with his teeth and pulled her along, rounding the curve of the inlet. The rainy season wasn't over, and the island was practically empty. He slid his cock under the edge of her nylon crotch, diving into her like a torpedo. Her suit snapped back around the base of his sex. She grasped his neck, and they sat. Teeter-totter. Pressed together in the water, rocking softly with a little tide. All of her pushed against him, humming and hanging on a spool of skin.

I love you, Quintana Roo.

SHARK STEW

Scientists gathered on the island. Healthy, attractive women and men, experts on sharks, a convivial group who'd traveled with Cousteau. They'd come to investigate a cave between the island and the mainland. Discovered by an abalone diver, it was filled with sharks who appeared to be asleep. Although it was believed that sharks never slept, the scientists anticipated that the cave's currents might be swift enough to move their gills while sleeping. With them was a film crew experienced in underwater techniques. The plan was to film divers as they entered the cave, swam up to a shark, and clubbed it on the snout, startling it from "sleep."

They wanted to include a pair of female tourists for atmosphere, a contrast to marine life. Annie and Ingrid would only have to wear scuba gear and go into the water.

"No problem," Annie said.

"No problem," Ingrid agreed.

On the day of the shoot, they motored out from Isla Mujeres towards Cancún. One of the crew strapped tanks on the women's back. And adjusted masks on their face, fins on their feet.

"Are there any instructions?"

"None," they said.

They opened the gate in the boat's railing.

The cameraman shouted, "Roll!"

Annie dove from the deck, the metal tank knocking the back of her head. Half-conscious, she sank. Dizzy, disoriented, in pain. Two team divers lifted her to the surface and carried her up the rope ladder to the deck.

"You're supposed to jump!"

"You're supposed to tell me!"

SLUT GODDESS

Unpredictably and from time to time, Annie became infatuated with hustlers or addicts, usually the combo, brilliant in their own way, who believed she was an ideal mate. They saw in her a young woman too pretty to be very smart and susceptible to persuasion, cajoling, flattery, pampering, conversion, and pressure. However, they were deceived. She wasn't fooled. But out of amusement, intrigue, curiosity, a lark, she let herself be seduced.

These were brief affairs with distinct similarities. They hated how she dressed in loose tunics and mannish shirts. They wanted her to flaunt her body. They tried to prove their superiority, usually in ridiculous ways. They never laughed at her jokes. They put her down. And were quick to cheat. Desire and rejection flipping as easily as a coin.

By contrast, her women friends were devoted, steadfast, and undemanding. Her mother asked her if she was a lesbian.

"I hope so," she said, trying to sound liberated and nonchalant. But her sexual encounters with women had been experimental, never motivated by lust.

There was an experience in college when a girl fell in love with her. Another on a bus when an older woman kissed her. Later when she lived in San Francisco, she went to lesbian clubs as a refuge from men. Fantastic places where women could drink and dance. And nobody tried to pick her up.

ONE EYE

On the coast natives watch the ships coming and going. They meet the invaders and conquerors. And centuries later, the carefree tourists. Hotels spring up. Beaches are overrun by travelers with money for vacations. They get jobs to serve the tourists. They depend on servile jobs and tips, and force themselves to be friendly. They note that a few pesos to buy a trinket or a blanket mean nothing to them. They tolerate the tradition of bargaining. A ritual which tourists insist upon for a few pesos. In turn, they try to con the tourists. And grow to hate and resent the outsiders.

In rural Mexico there is an old story that explains the bitterness of the poor.

Typically, a village had two rival wealthy families who required the loyalty of their peons. Such feuds led to years of spying, dueling, suicide, poison, and century-old quarrels over property, money, marriage, and inheritance. The origin of the dispute may have been forgotten, but it persisted universally from Verona to *Yojimbo*.

Two *campesinos* were returning from the fields when they saw Jesus walking towards them in a loincloth, His open wounds bleeding from His feet and hands. Awed, they crossed themselves and fell to the ground.

"I've come to give one of you whatever you wish," Jesus said.

The poor farmers could not believe their great fortune.

"And to the other, I'll give twice that."

Land, money, jewels, houses, there was no disagreement. But they argued who would ask first.

Jesus said when they were ready, they could find Him farther on the road.

They argued until sunset. Neither trusting the other's promise to split the difference. Then one took off running.

Jesus heard him. He stopped and waited, His expression as enigmatic as a crude colonial statue.

"My son, have you decided?"

Trembling, the peasant bowed and kissed Jesus's feet.

"*Sí! Sí! Sí! Sí! Sí!* That you put out one of my eyes!"

OAXACA TOWN

They arrived early in the morning after a bus ride through the mountains around harrowing hairpin curves with dozens of crosses that marked the spots of fatal accidents. Near the *zócalo* was a hotel with a vacant room. Check-in was afternoon, but a friendly couple approached them.

"Put your backpacks in our room," James and Lisa said.

Later, they retrieved their things with a promise to dine together. Conversation was lively. James circled the interesting local hamlets on their map: one that specialized in mezcal, another in belt weavers, a third with blanket weavers who reproduced twentieth-century masterpieces in wool by Picasso, Miro, Tanguy, Chagall.

Annie and Martin described the deserted roads from Yucatán to the lush foothills of Chiapas. Shrouded in trees and mist, Palenque was mystical, otherworldly, primordial. Unlike the mobs at Chichén Itzá and Uxmal, there were no other visitors. Sheer steps led up the exterior of the pyramid, sheer steps down into the moist crypt. Annie was frightened of heights. In her dreams of flying, there was always a parachute. Now she clasped the shriveled hand of the old caretaker. He was her parachute.

Most young Americans were lured to Palenque by psilocybin mushrooms and had never heard of the fabulous ruins. In the village were rumors that *federales* dressed like hippies to entrap them. Nobody knew who was who. Obsessed and paranoid, the foreigners wondered whether it was safe to harvest the mushrooms. And how to store them. Preserved in jars of honey was recommended.

At the campground in the middle of the night, an Arizona youth panicked that the *federales* were coming. He took off in his van, waking the other campers and howler monkeys, and leaving behind his clothes, a tent, and a camp stove.

Martin met a Mexican college student who offered to drive them into the countryside. In a grassy green pasture with Brahman cattle, they nibbled mushroom caps plucked from cow pies. A bull lifted its head and lowered it, signaling they should come so far and no farther. Soon the distant peaks and sky shimmered in bands of purple and gold. Their faces and the cattle shimmered, too. When it began to pour sheets of warm rain, their guide flung a woven poncho over himself. Martin unfolded a plastic rectangle into a jacket. Annie, however, was unprepared. Dressed in a flimsy cotton dress from the market in Mérida, she was rapidly soaked. She danced barefoot in the mud, falling and rolling with glee. A stoned comedy.

After dinner in Oaxaca's splendid *zócalo*, with its tall trees and arcades, they sat drinking coffee and sharing *regañadas*. Lisa was silent, chewing the ends of her waist-long hair. She was tired of travel stories. She didn't like that they talked about books she hadn't read. She thought her fiancé paid too much attention to Annie. It was he who suggested a word game, each of them sharing a favorite quote. Lisa balked. She didn't have a favorite quote. Annie had notebooks of them. Since childhood she'd written them down. Currently, she was reading César Vallejo, her brain filled with his poems.

"I'll go," James volunteered. "It's in French, you mind?"

"Annie speaks French," Martin said.

"*L'enfant abdique son extase.* Shall I translate?"

"I'm going back to the hotel," Lisa yawned.

Annie rose from the table. "I'll go with you."

The two women walked along the quiet, dark streets. Annie mumbling the line from Mallarmé scrawled on a page in her journal. *L'enfant abdique son extase.*

Had James rifled through her things? Did he mean to impress her? Or convey their mutual admiration of French poetry? Could it possibly be a coincidence? No, impossible!

"Will you marry him?"

"After the wedding we'll move to Toronto where James teaches."

"Do you trust him?" Annie whispered.

Lisa's eyes flamed. "Stay out of our business!"

In the morning they were gone.

She asked Martin if anything was missing from his backpack.

"Yeah," he said, "that naked photo of you."

SKIRTS AND SKINS

At Monte Albán the blocks of stone were massive, the view aerial. The amazement of the modern mind as it tries to fathom the machineless spectacle. Instead of wheels and engines, there were slaves. As Annie caressed the ancient carvings, Martin kissed her. His tongue diving into her mouth, tracing her gums, teasing her tongue deep inside his, and sucking ravenously. Attached like Olmec demons, they fell over the wall to the soft pad of grass. She pulled up her skirt and swung her legs around his back, her thighs locking his in a vice. Drawing the sap up the root to the trunk while the sky swelled with crimson clouds. They rocked across the sunset, listening to the whine of spirits and the yappy drone of a transistor radio.

Blood, sperm, semen, yeast.

NATURAL SELECTION

Feel along the bottom making sure it's not too soft. Find the center. It's the round entrance through the scaly folds. Push down on its softness. Not too juicy or too hard. Lop off the spiky bromeliad leaves and peel the outside. The tough skin leaves brown knots in the flesh. Slice into discs and sprinkle with cayenne. The song of sweet pineapple and hot chile makes your mouth beat.

In Bali the women warn not to eat pineapple. It makes the *bula* too juicy. Martin says there's no such thing as *too* juicy. Women's magazines say it's something to worry about. Three-year old Alexander declares, "I want to eat Thumbalina's *bula*."

She loves to see women feeling up fruit. Poking. Rubbing. Smelling. Cheese is more difficult. In France shoppers pinch the cheese. Michelle told her if you're looking for a good Camembert, press your eyelid. That's the way to gauge a Camembert. If it's softer, it's overripe.

On Saturday afternoon Annie and Nan walked to the movie theater. Whenever a car of grease balls drove by, they waved a banana out the window at them. The girls didn't understand what it meant, only that it was menacing and alluring.

Bananas, cucumbers, squash, pears, grapes. The shapes of things we love to eat. Cookie dough. Jars of pickled peaches. Cakes dusted with powdered sugar. Crisp bacon, berry jam, brown custard, shaved ice with syrup. The variety of beans in Mexico is astonishing. And exotic fruits that look like a monkey's rump.

In Oaxaca the market ladies scolded Annie for fondling the pineapples.

GETTING THE JUICE

Annie lay down on Jason's work table, her pants pulled to the middle of her thighs.

Michelle was with her. Laughing, smoking, drinking shots of rum like surgery without anesthesia. Jason turned on the drill and filled the tube. The noise came closer. Touchdown. She winced and took a breath. He stopped. The pain stopped. She relaxed. It wasn't so bad.

"That's the outline," he said, checking the illustration that Annie had brought with her. An image from Esther Harding's *Women's Mysteries*.

He refilled the drill and changed points.

Annie conjured buckets of warm ocean pouring over her. But it hurt like crazy. As bad as the jellyfish sting when she was four. Her father carried her out of the Atlantic to a shower on the beach, trying to scrub away the pain.

"Women tolerate it better than men. Men are crybabies," Jason said.

Michelle had a healer's touch. She held her palm above Annie's head.

"Remember when you stepped on a yellow jacket?"

Annie groaned. When it stung her arch, she felt electrified.

Satori. Safari. Salida. Jakarta. Jesus.

She loved tattoos and cheap hotels where everyone was either a resident or one-night stand. The bare rooms. The neon view and coarse yellowed sheets. The long hall, worn carpet, tattered wallpaper. The elaboration of love was immense in a room like that. The exhilaration of waking up with nothing except the clothes you wore and a carnival love-ride. You got up, left the bed unmade, and went out for the over-easy.

CRUEL AND USUAL

Martin looked bored as if they'd known each other for years instead of a few passionate months.

"Order me the shrimp," Annie said, whipping out the door to the zócalo. From every corner came men's hisses to get her attention. She hated the hissing. She hated Martin, too.

Last night at the bar the way he laughed with that pretty French girl. How old could she be? Sixteen? Where were her parents? He never laughs like that with me.

She arranged the shrimp and rice in piles. Feeling abandoned and replaced. Furious that she'd given him so much power and determined to recoup it.

"I have an appointment this afternoon," he said casually.

"Oh, really?"

"Ernesto with the boat," he lied.

"Ernesto?" she goaded.

"Maybe he'll take us fishing."

Am I supposed to think that's okay? If he lies to me? If he prefers her company to mine? If he wants to fuck her? Or was it her own fault for claiming to be the new feminist woman: liberated, unconventional, detached?

I'm not! I'm not! I'm not!

TROUBLE AND TROUBLEMAKER

"You're not eating," Martin said, taking her hand.

"No," she said, snatching it away.

Her bad mood wasn't his problem. In an hour he had a date to meet a French girl. *Très mignonne*, exactly his type. A reminder to Annie that he was doing what he wanted. If the girl proved slightly interesting, he'd continue doing it. Even to himself he sounded like a jerk. But it couldn't be helped. At times everyone was a jerk.

I could skip the date, he thought. *And go back to the hotel. Wasn't lovemaking why siesta was invented? After lunch Annie's favorite hour, not so energetic as morning or enervating as night. Later, we'd wander to the beach, sit with tequila and limes, and watch the sun sink into the water. I'd finger her between her legs, grip her spongy nipple between my lips, cup her bottom.*

He sat on the creaky restaurant toilet, smoking and ruminating, tumescent with fantasies of two women in one afternoon. As his excitement increased, it was interrupted by the smirk of Jerry. Pesky Jerry whom he'd seen in the Jardín Álvaro Obregon that morning. Wherever they went, there was Jerry. A yahoo college boy and his cohort of obnoxious friends. Mérida. Isla Mujeres. San Cristóbal. Lake Atitlán. Oaxaca. And now Manzanillo.

Lake Atitlán had been the highpoint of the trip. A caldera at five thousand feet with three volcanoes sparkling over its deep blue water and a dozen Mayan villages dotting its thirty-mile circumference. Some you could walk to. For others it was easy to hire locals to row you in their *pirogue*.

Panajachel was where most tourists stayed. Among them Jerry, stoned on codeine-laced Robitussin and ludes, drinking noisily, and parading nude in the tree-lined shoals of the lake where native women routinely bathed.

Unintentionally, Martin and Annie teamed up with him to hike to a famous waterfall. Through the jungle and clearings of banana and coffee plantations without roads or signs, they got lost. But when they finally reached the falls, awaiting them was a spectacular vista of cataract and pools. As the river was extremely low, rather than negotiate the steep ridge on their side, Jerry charged ahead, wading into the water towards the far bank. A few steps in, he was swept away by the deceptive undercurrent. With his hand clinging to a rock, he dangled from the precipice.

Everybody froze. Seconds passed. But when reality sank in, there was anger and dismay. His drugged madness had put them all in peril. Two of his friends, unquestionably high, went into the river to coach him. But Jerry wasn't strong or acrobatic. He couldn't swing himself over the lip of the falls. For another minute he held on. But he couldn't hold on indefinitely. Looking at a man hanging over a cliff was looking at death. Low water meant dangerous rocks below.

One friend holding onto another, Martin wading in, Annie following, and the others made a human chain across the river. They managed to grab Jerry's leg and drag him to safety.

Now Martin and Annie were Jerry's saviors. He was their bad luck charm.

FARAWAY

The town was quiet. Siesta. The shops closed except a gift store and tourist café. She waited at the corner. The rickety bus stank of diesel. Mexico stank of diesel. They sped through the town's center to the outskirts, jostling past fields, huts, banana trees, and canopies of bougainvillea. Clotheslines flashed by. Children waved. Buzzards clung to a carcass in the middle of the road. She loved the tropics. Half fecund, half decay.

On the bus two large women embraced a sleeping child on their laps. A tableau of Diego Rivera. A withered man with cloudy eyes. Another Rivera. A handsome youth, dark and round featured, sat next to her. An *indio* with ropey muscles and burnt caramel skin. Rivera everywhere.

She hoped her note had irritated Martin. She hoped she ruined his afternoon. However, her nasty mood had passed. She was faraway. Her mind a hotline to New Mexico and the dry purple ground. Her friend Molly on the mesa with goats and a baby while she rolled through Eden, happy to be alone.

Molly's labor was average for a first baby. Seventeen hours. She'd had him at home. Annie was there. The early hours fun and games, singing show tunes and playing rummy. By dawn things weren't fun anymore. Annie called Molly's midwife. In New Mexico midwifery was legal. In California it was still risky business. A midwife had recently been arrested by one of her patients. A pregnant undercover cop.

Annie and the midwife massaged Molly's coccyx to relieve the pressure. Back labor. And her abdomen, hoping the baby would turn. Molly moaned. Annie and the midwife moaned with her. A chorus of moans. Thankfully, they weren't in a hospital. Natural childbirth books said you had to be cool in a hospital. Or at least, sound cool. Molly wasn't cool at all.

She tried to get out of bed, but what she really wanted was to get out of her body. She rolled to the rug, then stood. Her waters burst, amniotic skim spreading over the floor. She said she couldn't go on. She bit Tom's hand and slapped him. She sank to the floor. And repeated she couldn't go on although she had no choice. Childbirth is its own imperative, overtaking will and negation of will.

Thirty minutes later, Billy Bumper Jack Prince of the Rodeo was born. Molly leapt up like a mare. She took a shower while Annie changed the sheets. The midwife put the placenta in the fridge. She rinsed the umbilicus and put it in the fridge, too. They sat on the bed, eating fried chicken and drinking champagne, Molly holding the holy newborn. Molly Madonna.

The bus turned. A small bay came into view. A few nets on the sand, a few boats at the dock. A shack for cold drinks and snacks. Palm trees for shade. Perfection.

FATA MORGANA

The senses are more fickle than the heart. Their generosity makes us twist and dive to get at them again. Smell the coffee. Smell the squealing tires. Smell the tomato leaf. Smell your own smell before you get your monthly bleed. Smell sweat.

Now see. What do you see? The painted tiles. The pitched roofs. The window in the eave. The curtain in the window. The gleam of lamp in the curtain. And behind a thousand veils. Winesburg, Ohio. The road to Mandalay. Kwaidan. The Golden Section. And the big Big Dipper. Dip dip dipping. The stuff of our being. The framework of fact.

Whistle, and I'll come. Sing, and I'll dance. Crunch. Yell. Chomp. Grunt. Whimper. Sigh. Howl at the blue moon. Gregorian chants. Gershwin rhapsodies. Sax solos. Delta blues. Wind chimes. Heavy rain. Falling rocks. And the absolute silence of snow.

Sensorial. Risqué. Sensual love. *Baby, baby, baby! You know what I like!*

Those brows. That voice. Those hands. That back. Those thighs. That neck. Those breasts. That tongue. Those teeth. Dimples, freckles, winks, smiles. At the gas station the way they smile. *Fill her up, ma'am?* That chest. Those feet. That fur. Those paws. That tail. That beak. Phantasmagoric. The body. Standing. Walking. Lying. Squatting. Trotting. Humping. Pinching. Stroking. Don't stop. Don't ever stop.

On the Paris Metro his eye bolted hers through the glass. Airtight. Shut out. Train east. Train west. Trains stopped. An instantaneous explosion. Love travels the speed of light. What did he look like, the lover who blew her a kiss before he sped away?

The French inspire such things.

And all of us? Us the Chinese. The Masai. The Kiwanis. The yogis. The cool cat. The big dog. The dumb ass. We have our inspirations. From blue cheese and ocean tides. From foxes in heat. Mown grass. Horse dung. Fresh juice. Forest green. Venetian red. Rose gold. Black pearl.

Chemicals have done a lot to change our faces. TV is plastic surgery.

Get it! I can eat this rug! And you, too. You're so sweet, I can eat you up.

POISON GAS

The bugs are ferocious in San Blas, especially mosquitos and *jejenes*. Bad for tourists but a feast for birds. San Blas is a bird paradise. And attracts birders from all over. They drift on boats through the swamp, surrounded by hundreds of bird species and the songs of thousands. From the river's mouth to a fresh spring, passing eerie mazes of mangroves, their wide, stiff roots and trunks like ghostly farthingales.

In the campground they tied their hammocks between the palms. They strung their box-shaped mosquito nets with sticks through the ropes of the hammock. The nets were gauzy mesh, ingenious and bug proof, and enveloped them in a cocoon. Sleeping, Annie was transported to a seraglio in *Arabian Nights*.

She was ecstatic to return to the beach, away from the polluted cities, the hissing men, the hordes of beggars, and the walls of the rich capped with broken glass. She changed into a bathing suit, a white diaphanous shirt, and the *huaraches* she'd bought in Guadalajara. After soaking them in water, she let them dry on her feet. They fit perfectly.

The sea was a sheet of blue moire silk. She jumped over the light breakers and swam far from shore. She emerged from the surf like "The Birth of Venus." Sometimes she imagined herself in a painting. Not from vanity but rather the feelings that paintings aroused inside her. She was introduced to Botticelli during a winter in Florence when entry to the Uffizi was free, the *salas* empty, and the guards her friends.

On the beach Martin had a new companion. Together, they watched Annie saunter towards them: her long, wet ringleted hair, her glistening skin, her jade eyes aglow.

The bearded German ex-pat pumped her hand and doffed his straw sombrero. Tanned and rotund with a shelf for a midriff that dwarfed his spindly legs, he jumped up. From a *palapa* he brought chips and a Fanta for Annie. He had lived in San Blas for ten years.

"As a child I heard them talk about Jewish women. 'The most

beautiful women in the world,' they said." Smiling,"I never knew it was true before."

Before what? Before your fathers and uncles murdered them all?

Annie's joy evaporated. All six months of it.

"I'm sick," she told Martin.

"You must drink," the German said.

When he felt her forehead, she recoiled. But she didn't hit him. At Lake Atitlán she'd shocked herself by hitting an adolescent. A boy who squatted on the beach near her, stuttering English phrases. She ignored him, but he came closer. He touched her, and she socked his arm. A pathetic scapegoat for men who assumed a solo woman wanted company.

"I have to lie down," she said.

"Take the Fanta," the German said.

"No!" Anything from him was poison.

She gathered her towel and book. And leaned on Martin's shoulder.

"Auf wiedersehen!" the German shouted cheerfully as they strolled away.

HIJACKED

A caravan of two vans, two trucks, and a Land Rover invaded the campground. All of them new white vehicles with California license plates and logos of a mermaid inscribed with "Diving Dolls." Along with diving instructors, a small film crew, and equipment that included a shark cage and cartons of canned food and drinks, there were a dozen women from Los Angeles who'd been recruited for an adventure in Yucatán.

The boss was Ronald, a porn mogul who wanted to make an arty film about girls and sharks. Ronald had a list of rules: no eating Mexican food, no speaking to Mexicans, no leaving camp without permission. The "dolls" (a few over 40) were permitted to go out as a group, dressed in a uniform of polo shirts with a mermaid and the insignia "Diving Dolls" and navy skirts or shorts. Comporting themselves politely was also a rule. No swearing although Ronald swore every other word.

He said to Martin, "I could use a couple of brains on the trip to doctor the script and write promo for the film."

Paid to ride through Mexico, what could be the downside? Martin and Annie packed up their campsite and stored the car and gear with Jens, a Swede living on his sailboat.

The "dolls" rode in the vans except for Ronald's girlfriend Cherie. She rode with him in the Land Rover outfitted with a stereo tape deck, a bar fridge, a cooler of poppers, and a walkie talkie system. Cherie was the prettiest of the lot with a snub nose and blond bob, possessing an abundance of positivity. A transplant from Des Moines to Hollywood, an aspiring actress, and now fucking a *real* film producer. Annie and Martin rode with them.

Off they went, the Rover in the lead. Hours passed without incident until they reached a tollbooth where Ronald explained in English that he'd pay for the trucks and vans behind him. When the tolltaker didn't *comprende*, Ronald stepped out from the Rover with a baseball bat and yelled, "You dumb fuck Mexican!" A real maniac. They were waved through gratis.

Afterwards, Annie opted to ride with the "dolls." They'd answered a newspaper ad: ATTRACTIVE WOMEN NEEDED FOR FREE EXCURSION TO MEXICO AND LEGITIMATE MOVIE. Some wanted a chance to act, others an escapade. They all admitted they were running away from either a boyfriend, debt, or the law. Their agreement required them to give their passports to Ronald, which meant no one could leave at will. Those who tried were told they'd signed a contract. An inviolable contract.

Except for rest stops and meals of canned corn, canned beans, crackers, and soda, they pushed on to Mexico City. The plan was to spend a night in the capital before heading east. They secured the vehicles in the parking lot of a stylish Holiday Inn where Ronald had booked a dozen rooms. Annie and Martin opted to sleep in a van.

At midnight they heard pounding on the van's door. "Help me!" a woman cried.

It was Cherie. Ronald had punched her after he discovered her in the hotel bar with an American Airlines pilot. Definitely against the rules. He threw her around, bloodied her nose, blackened her eye. She notified the front desk who promised to call the police.

Ronald trotted into the parking lot after her, partially dressed and holding his duffle. He jumped into the Land Rover, popped a vial of amyl nitrate, and turned on the walkie talkie.

"Pack the fuck up! We're getting the fuck out of here!"

He wanted nothing to do with the Mexican police. He was a convicted felon in California and violating parole. He could be arrested for assault and deported to face charges in the U.S.

"I'm not going!" Cherie said.

"You're going!" Ronald said.

By now the other "dolls" were in the parking lot wrapped in hotel blankets. They said they weren't going either. They demanded their passports. Ronald complied, but for the girls with no money, they were stuck. Minutes later, the caravan vanished into the dark streets of the city.

Annie, Martin, and Cherie spent the night in the bus station. They bought three tickets to San Blas, and by the next evening they were back at their campsite by the river where life was simple. When Annie and Martin left to go north, Cherie stayed on. She and Jens had fallen in love and planned to sail to Tahiti.

HIGHWAY ROBBERY

Outside Tepic they picked up newlyweds from Montreal, who'd hitchhiked as far south as Panama on their honeymoon. An hour later there was a roadblock. A shiny pickup and a dilapidated car crossed the blacktop, guarded by four men in jeans, cowboy hats, tooled leather boots, and holding 12-gauge shotguns.

"Federales," their chief said.

It wasn't obvious they were *federales*. They wore no badges, and their vehicles had no official markings. They were undoubtedly *bandidos*, infamous on roads where tourists traveled.

"*Cuanto pasar?*" the Canadian asked.

"We see!" they said, herding Martin and company out of the car with their guns.

The search for *contrabando* took a long time. The longer it took, the more apparent it became that something would turn up. They found a roach in *Mexico on 5 Dollars a Day* and Annie's jar of honey and mushrooms.

The *jefe* rubbed his thumb over his index finger, the international sign for cash.

"We have no money," Martin said.

"*Mala suerte!*" he laughed.

A hundred dollars for each man and sex with the women. The Canadian gave them two hundred dollars which canceled the sex. After arguing, Martin handed them his grandfather's Omega watch. Annie lay in the cab of the truck. She closed her eyes and gritted her teeth, counting. Less than 200 seconds and it was over.

"You're a champ," Martin said.

"I never want to fuck again," Annie said.

They reached Mazatlán on Christmas Eve. Midnight mass in the cathedral and a bullfight on Christmas Day. They bought tickets for *sol* seats crowded with rowdy local families and hampers of food and drink. They were the only Americans. In Mallorca Annie had seen El Cordobés, a master of elegance and bravura. By comparison Mexican matadors were notorious for botched finales.

She was sad to leave Mexico. She cried as they drove to the ferry for La Paz. Beside the dock a young man sprawled on the pavement. A heap of emaciated limbs in rags.

"I want to give him something," she said to Martin.

It was a *huipil* from Chichi. One of the stained *huipils* that were sometimes dyed in coffee and sold to tourists. She preferred them to the new ones.

As soon as she placed it on him, the man clawed her arm. "*Puta! Puta!*" He spit and hurled the garment back at Annie. From the deck of the ferry, she could hear him. "*Puta! Puta! Puta!*"

INCHES AND LIVES

The yard in New Mexico was full of clay. Kaolin. To loosen the soil, they had to haul in a truckload of sawdust and chicken manure. It was hard work to ready the ground. They fashioned scarecrows from scrap metal like Paolo Soleri's bell trees in the desert at Arcosanti. It was going to be a big garden with squash, chile, melons, and beans.

Plant seeds one inch deep, eight seeds per foot in a row.

Farmers recommended that the best way to keep crows away from crops was to kill one and hang it in a tree. But Annie liked the crows who wintered in the cottonwoods.

Seeds germinate in nine to fifteen days.

Her period was late. That wasn't unusual. Traveling confused her body. But things had started to smell funny, both aromatic and gross. She craved pastrami, and cilantro made her vomit.

A urine test confirmed that she was pregnant. She left the clinic in shock. Walking outside anywhere in New Mexico was a shock. The blinding sun and blinding sky.

When seedlings are two inches tall, thin or transplant to three inches apart.

She went back to the clinic to telephone Martin. No answer. Maybe he was at the bar. The Thunderbird Bar. The baby. The baby bar. The candy bar. The Baby Ruth. The baseball star. The bat. The baby. Inside her.

Tie plants to trellis or support. Thrives in non-acid amended soil with good drainage.

She drove north and up the mountain to Placitas. If Martin wasn't there, there was Dede Lee. Or Tom and Molly might be home.

Boy. Girl. Tender tiny pussy cock. Family. Darling. Baby bunny.

In rows three feet apart.

She said she'd always be ready to have an abortion. Every woman's right. No more unwanted kids to grow into unwanted adults. Wanting.

Unwanting. Womb. Room. Warp. Loom. Weft. Bereft. She couldn't feel the tiny bean buried in her female loam. Soiled and spoiled. A garden going to waste. They didn't want a baby. Not now. Not her.

Martin showed her a postcard from Papeete. Cherie was pregnant and if it was a girl, Anna Martine would be her name.

Cherie had written, *You saved me!*

"Sweet," Annie said, ordering a Coke and a bag of chips. Her go-to for the four basic food groups: sugar, salt, caffeine, and fat. "And a shot of brandy," she added.

"Special occasion?" Martin grinned.

"I just came from the clinic."

"And what!"

I'm pregnant, Martin! Pregnant, pregnant, categorically pregnant!

"Kiss me, Annie! And drinks on the house!"

She put her head down on the bar and wept.

The nurse offered her a sedative. Penance or pride, she chose to suffer. She lay on the exam table, her feet in the cold stirrups, under a blanket and shaking with cold. Beside her was the vacuum machine. And as the hose went into her, there was a loud swooshing noise. The pain was torture. Like something being taken out that didn't want to go. Like abalone from its shell. Or a walnut that has to be picked. Or mosses on rocks. Honey in combs. Tangles in hair. Pomegranate seeds. Something stubborn and content. Her body stung. All of her ached. Empty and fallow again.

SEVENTH HEAVEN

You choose a spot. An unlikely spot. An incongruous and divine spot. Something with a little rhythm like an elevator. Like the swoon in your belly on a fast elevator. Like the way the swoon dives into your groin.

They're riding up the Campanile past landings with slabs of carved stones, an armadillo, a marble column. At the top is a narrow walkway. And an arch with carillon chimes. Annie flattens herself against the wall. Their jeans unzipped. Her long winter coat around them. She watches San Francisco flicker in and out of fog. Like shadows on the quays of Paris. *Au quai*. F-stop. A quick fuck.

Change the spot. The man. The speed. Is that what the senses desire? Shove. Force. Break. Erupt. Quake. Something pushed into something else. Tongue and groove. Squeezed into the anus. Pressing the womb with rectal skin. Go slow. Use Vaseline. Olive oil. Crisco. Butter. *Why shouldn't it feel good?* With lots of spit. Grease and polish. The fluted crown. The other side of the moon.

During the Sylmar earthquake, Annie was knocked out of bed at dawn in a house of glass and steel. Built in the 50s to be quake-proof, everything rattled but nothing broke. Not a dish or a glass. On the patio the fishpond sloshed like high tide. Gas lines and sunrise ignited the horizon. The Great Mother groaned.

Bowels of the Earth
Blessings from the Sky

WAIST DOWN

Life becomes more strange and less surprising. Sex is exactly the reverse.

Messy hair. Limp wrist. Sated eye. Hungry mouth. Sweet lips. Sour tongue.

You have to find out what it is. You have to practice. Then you have to let it go.

He dove for the bed. She ducked and ran. He caught her wrist. She hammered him with her fist. It felt good to be overcome. To laugh. Resist. Give in. She collapsed on his chest. They lay on the floor. Her insides beating like wings.

I love you. I love you. I love you. I love you. I love you.

People believe love is a fixed point. In the future or in the past. For a second or two, almost everyone I've ever loved I wished were dead . . . because I felt dead myself. It's okay to have sick thoughts. You have them and let them go. Or risk their overtaking you with a life of their own.

We go along. Along and along. Headlong. Neck up. Chest down. Eyes open. Eyes shut. Back bent or straight. Bumping to a great standup bass. A guitar with a missing string. A cane flute. An orgasmic sax. Maybe it's the way her thigh crosses his. And that's what the lowlife is doing tonight, every foot tapping, tipping, grinding, shuffling, sliding.

As for the upper half, it's breathing, listening, looking, expiring while the head makes a zillion calculations. Waiting for the dial tone. She can remember how they met but not what she remembered then. She can remember what she forgot but only if she remembers to remember it.

They have a holding pattern. They want to work it out. But also they wonder if they'll stay together.

Isn't it beautiful here?

It is beautiful here.

The way the wooden boats glide over the lake. The deep blue water and the mountains silhouetted on the deep blue sky. The dazzling sun and starlight.

Everything reminds me of everything, and that's why in some way, sex is always on my mind.

we are climbing up a steep hill
a steep hill and it is dangerous
dangerous and rocky and the
climb is exceedingly difficult
and very narrow in parts with
large boulders to walk around
and very dry and we are thirsty
but we want to get to the top
and you give me your hand and
help me through the hardest parts
and then we are at the top and
it's a small mountain town
very white with huge cactuses
and blossoming vines

to the left through the spaces
between the white houses and
rock walls is the facade of
an enormous church
and a view of a city far away
with an odd perspective
we know it is far off
even though it looks close
gigantically close
it's not a real city
but a painting
proportioned in
the style of Uccello

we stand in the middle of
the square with the feeling
of heaven over us and then
you put your arms around me
and hold me and say it's good
to be here with you
it's good to be. . . .

A word of gratitude to friends, family, and colleagues who supported these works in various ways: Ella Baff, Susan Banyas, Beau Beausoleil, Gillian Boal, Felix Brenner, Jackie Patterson Brenner, James Brook, Ignacio Chapela, Agnès Douillet, Gloria Frym, Cassell Gross, Lianne Halfon, Nancy Key, Katrine Le Gallou, Joanna Bean Martin, Nancy Peters, Amelie Prescott, Mo Slotin, Cosette Thompson, Jacquelyn West, Geoff Young—and a very special thanks to Iain Boal for his eagle eye and Laura Chester for her commitment to the original version of *The Soft Room*.

SUMMER BRENNER was raised in Georgia and migrated east first to New England and Europe, and then west to New Mexico and eventually Berkeley where she has been a long-time resident. She has published a dozen works of fiction, poetry, and novels for youth. Her papers are available in Special Collections at the University of Delaware.

LEWIS WARSH (1944-2020) is the author of over thirty volumes of poetry, fiction and autobiography, including *Out of the Question: Selected Poems 1963-2003* (Station Hill, 2017), *One Foot Out the Door: Collected Stories* (Spuyten Duyvil, 2014), *A Place in the Sun* (Spuyten Duyvil, 2010) and *Inseparable: Poems 1995-2005* (Granary Books, 2008). He was co-founder, with Bernadette Mayer, of United Artists Magazine and Books. He taught at Naropa University, The Poetry Project, SUNY Albany, Bowery Poetry and Long Island University, where he was director of the MFA program in creative writing from 2007-2013.